SECOND

ALL ABOUT THE USA 1

A Cultural Reader

Milada Broukal

PEARSON
Longman

All About the USA 1: A Cultural Reader, Second Edition

Pearson Education, 10 Bank Street, White Plains, NY 10606

Staff credits: The people who made up the *All About the USA 1* team, representing editorial, production, design, and manufacturing, are: Wendy Campbell, Nan Clarke, Dave Dickey, Laura LeDréan, Melissa Leyva, Robert Ruvo, Paula Van Ells and Pat Wosczyk

Photo credits: p.14 © James Randklev/Corbis; **p.18** (first) Index Stock/Alamy, (second) MPI/Getty Images, (third) ML Harris/Getty Images, (fourth) Food Features/Alamy, (fifth) © Bettmann/Corbis, (sixth) © Bettmann/Corbis, (seventh) © Bettmann/Corbis, (eighth) National Library of Medicine; **p.19** (first) ilian studio/Alamy, (second) Stockbyte Silver/Alamy; **p.30** National Library of Medicine; **p.34** (first) © Redfx/Alamy, (second) © Lake County Museum/Corbis, (third) George Marks/Getty Images, (fourth) © Envision/Corbis, (fifth) Helene Rogers/Alamy, (sixth) Michael Gilday/Alamy; **p.35** (first) Blend Images/Alamy, (second) © William Gottlieb/Corbis, (third) Associated Press, (fourth) © Underwood & Underwood/Corbis, (fifth) © Bo Zaunders/Corbis, (sixth) © James Leynse/Corbis; **p.36** © Bo Zaunders/Corbis; **p.45** © James Leynse/Corbis; **p.50** (first) © Leng/Leng/Corbis, (second) Tony Lilley/Alamy, (third) Kitt Cooper-Smith/Alamy, (fourth) © Justin Lane/epa/Corbis, (fifth) JupiterImages/Comstock Images/Alamy, (sixth) © Lee Snider/PhotoImages/Corbis; **p.51** (first) Jon Arnold Images/Alamy, (second) © Bettmann/Corbis, (third) Daniel Dempster Photography/Alamy, (fourth) © William Manning/Corbis, (fifth) © Joe McDonald/Corbis, (sixth) © Kelly Redinger/Design Pics/Corbis, (seventh) © PictureNet/Corbis; **p.52** Ericka McConnell/Getty Images; **p.56** © Justin Lane/epa/Corbis; **p.60** © Bettmann/Corbis; **p.64** (first) © Bettmann/Corbis, (second) © Medio Images/Corbis, (third) © William Manning/Corbis, (fourth) Digital Vision/Getty Images; **p.65** (first) © Atlantide Phototravel/Corbis, (second) Jon Arnold Images/Alamy, (third) © MedioImages/Corbis, (fourth) Rolf Richardson/Alamy; **p.66** © MedioImages/Corbis; **p.70** © Bettmann/Corbis; **p.75** © William Manning/Corbis; **p.80** (first) Richard Howard/Getty Images, (second) Anatoly Pronin/Alamy, (third) Mike Dobel/Alamy, (fourth) Associated Press; **p.81** (first) © Bettmann/Corbis, (second) © Corbis, (third) © Mitchell Gerber/Corbis, (fourth) © Bettmann/Corbis, (fifth) © Bettmann/Corbis, (sixth) Katy Winn/Corbis, (seventh) Walt Disney/The Kobal Collection, (eighth) © Michael Ochs Archives/Corbis; **p.82** Walt Disney/The Kobal Collection; **p.87** Richard Howard/Getty Images; **p.91** © Bettmann/Corbis; **p.96** (first) © Archivo Iconografico, SA/Corbis, (second) © Bettmann/Corbis, (third) © Museum of the City of New York/Corbis; **p.97** (first) © Bettmann/Corbis, (second) MPI/Getty Images, (third) Henry Guttmann/Getty Images; **p.98** © Archivo Iconografico, SA/Corbis; **p.106** Henry Guttmann/Getty Images

Illustrations: Jill Wood

Text composition: Integra

Text font: 12/15 New Aster

Library of Congress Cataloging-in-Publication Data
Broukal, Milada.
  All about the USA / Milada Broukal.— 2nd ed.
      p. cm.
  Rev. ed. of: All about the USA, 1st ed. 1999.
  Revised ed. will be published in 4 separate volume levels.
  ISBN 0-13-613892-6 (student bk. with audio cd v. 1, : alk. paper)
  ISBN 0-13-240628-4 (student bk. with audio cd v. 2, : alk. paper)
  ISBN 0-13-234969-8 (student bk. with audio cd v. 3, : alk. paper)
  ISBN 0-13-234968-X (student bk. with audio cd v. 4, : alk. paper)
  1. Readers—United States.   2. English language—Textbooks for foreign
speakers.   3. United States—Civilization—Problems, exercises, etc.
  I. Murphy, Peter (Peter Lewis Keane), 1947-   II. Milhomme, Janet.
  III. Title.
  PE1127.H5B68 2008
  428.64—dc22

                                                                              2007032614

ISBN-10: 0-13-613892-6
ISBN-13: 978-0-13-613892-1

Printed in the United States of America
1 2 3 4 5 6 7 8 9 10—CRK—12 11 10 09 08 07

CONTENTS

INTRODUCTION

ALL ABOUT THE USA 1 is a low-beginning reader for English language students. It is divided into seven general knowledge areas, which are presented with colorful art and an optional culture quiz. Each part has three units that introduce typical American people, places, and things, providing students with essential information about the USA and stimulating cross-cultural exchange. The vocabulary and structures used in the text have been carefully controlled to help students gain fluency and confidence.

Each unit contains:
- An opening photo and prereading questions
- A short reading passage
- Topic-related vocabulary work
- Comprehension of main ideas
- Comprehension of details
- An Interactive Activity
- A Writing activity
- *A Did You Know...?* section offering a fun fact about the topic

The **PREREADING** questions are linked to the photo on the first page of each unit. They focus the students on the topic of the unit by introducing names, encouraging speculation about content, involving the students' own experiences when possible and presenting vocabulary as the need arises.

The **READING** passage for each unit ranges from about 200 to about 250 words. Students should first skim the passage for a general idea of the content. The teacher may wish to deal with some of the vocabulary at this point. The students should then read the passage carefully as they listen to the audio CD. Listening while reading helps students to comprehend and retain information in the reading.

The **VOCABULARY** exercise focuses on the boldfaced words in the reading and is designed to help students become more self-reliant by encouraging them to work out the meanings from the context.

There are two **COMPREHENSION** exercises. *Looking for Main Ideas* should be used in conjunction with the text to help students develop reading skills, and not as a test of memory. Students are asked to confirm the basic content of the text, which they can do individually, in pairs, in small groups, or as a whole class. *Looking for Details* expands the students' exploration of the text, concentrating on the scanning skills necessary to derive maximum value from reading.

The **ACTIVITY** section personalizes a theme related to the reading, encouraging students to share their own ideas or knowledge with their classmates.

The **WRITING** section prompts students to write simple sentences about a subject related to the topic of the unit. Teachers should use their own judgment when deciding whether to correct the writing exercises.

PART 1

THE UNITED STATES

Unit 1 Florida
Unit 2 Washington
Unit 3 Vermont

Mt. St. Helens is an active volcano.

Washington

CANADA

Mt. Rushmore i a mountain wit the faces of fou presidents.

Olympia

Helena

North Dako

Montana

Bismarck

Salem

Idaho

South Dakota

Oregon

Boise

Pierre

POTATOES

Wyoming

Nebraska

Cheyenne

Sacramento

Salt Lake City

Carson City

Utah

Denver

Kan

Nevada

California

Colorado

The Golden Gate Bridge is in San Francisco.

Santa Fe

Phoenix

New Mexico

Arizona

Texas

PACIFIC OCEAN

Millions of people visit the Grand Canyon every year.

MEXICO

U.S. FACTS

There are 50 states in the United States.

Each of the 50 states has a state capital where its government meets.

Delaware was the 1st state.

Hawaii was the 50th state.

About 300 million people live in the United States.

The United States has more corn ,

beef , and

milk than any other

country.

Honolulu

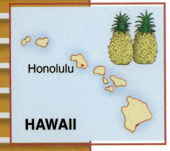

HAWAII

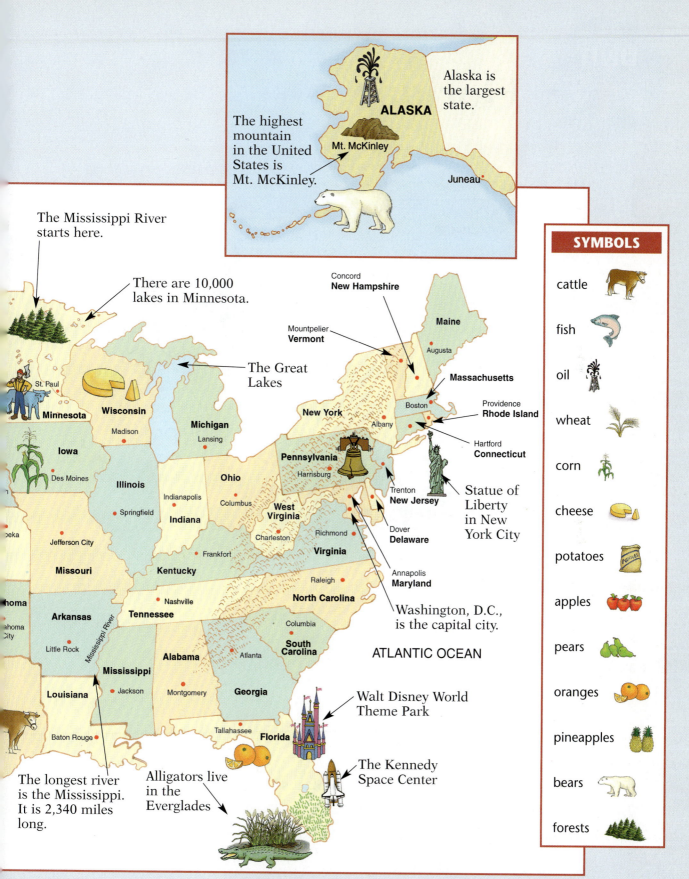

The highest mountain in the United States is Mt. McKinley.

ALASKA

Alaska is the largest state.

Mt. McKinley

Juneau

The Mississippi River starts here.

There are 10,000 lakes in Minnesota.

Concord
New Hampshire

Mountpelier
Vermont

Maine

Augusta

The Great Lakes

Massachusetts

New York

Boston

St. Paul

Wisconsin

Minnesota

Madison

Michigan

Lansing

Albany

Providence
Rhode Island

Hartford
Connecticut

Iowa

Illinois

Pennsylvania

Harrisburg

Trenton
New Jersey

Statue of Liberty in New York City

Des Moines

Indianapolis

Columbus

Ohio

Springfield

Indiana

West Virginia

Charleston

Richmond

Dover
Delaware

Jefferson City

Frankfort

Virginia

Missouri

Kentucky

Annapolis
Maryland

peka

Raleigh

Washington, D.C., is the capital city.

ahoma

ahoma
City

Arkansas

Little Rock

Tennessee

Nashville

North Carolina

Columbia

South Carolina

ATLANTIC OCEAN

Mississippi

Alabama

Atlanta

Louisiana

Jackson

Montgomery

Georgia

Baton Rouge

Tallahassee

Florida

Walt Disney World Theme Park

The Kennedy Space Center

The longest river is the Mississippi. It is 2,340 miles long.

Alligators live in the Everglades

To quiz yourself about **THE UNITED STATES**, go to page 111.

SYMBOLS

cattle

fish

oil

wheat

corn

cheese

potatoes

apples

pears

oranges

pineapples

bears

forests

Florida

TALLAHASSEE

Walt Disney World Theme Park

Kennedy Space Center

FLORIDA

Everglades

PREREADING

Answer the questions.

1. Why do people like to live in warm places?

2. Why do tourists like to go to Florida?

3. What do you know about Disney World?

Florida

Welcome to Florida, the "Sunshine State." If you like warm weather, Florida is the best place for a vacation. Millions of visitors come to Florida each year. They like its **sandy beaches**, **theme parks**, and natural beauty.

Miami is a big tourist city. People love its beautiful beaches. There are many coconut **palm trees** along the streets and beaches in Miami. They are very pretty. They are also dangerous! People work as coconut watchers. They make sure that coconuts do not fall on the tourists' heads!

Florida is famous for its theme parks. The world's largest theme park is Walt Disney World, near Orlando. A train takes people around Disney World. One part, the EPCOT Center, is all about the future. You can see life, food, and transportation in the future.

Florida has other things to see, too. You can go to the Kennedy Space Center. This is where **astronauts** go up into space. You can see how astronauts study space. If you go south, you can see wildlife in the Everglades. The Everglades is an area of some land and a lot of water. Grass grows in the water. Many wild animals such as **alligators** live in this **swamp**.

Millions of tourists come to Florida for a vacation. Many people come to Florida to live, too. Older people from cold states come to relax in the sunshine. Young people come to Florida, too. Florida has many new kinds of jobs. Florida has something for everyone.

VOCABULARY

Match the words and the pictures. Write your answer on the line.

sandy beaches	palm trees	alligator
theme park	astronauts	~~swamp~~

1. ___swamp___

2. _____

3. _____

4. _____

5. _____

6. _____

COMPREHENSION

⭐ UNDERSTANDING THE MAIN IDEA

Circle the letter of the best answer.

1. People like to visit Florida because ____.

    a. there are many things to see and do

    b. there are many jobs for young people

    c. visitors can learn how to become astronauts

2. Many older people live in Florida because ____.

    a. there are theme parks to visit

    b. the weather is warm

    c. there are many kinds of fruits to eat

LOOKING FOR DETAILS

Complete each sentence with the correct word or words. Write the letter of your answer on the line.

1. Florida is famous for its __d__.
2. Florida is called the "Sunshine State" because of its ____.
3. The EPCOT Center is all about the ____.
4. At the Kennedy Space Center, you can see how ____ study space.
5. There are ____ in the Everglades.

a. astronauts
b. future
c. warm weather
d. theme parks
e. alligators

ACTIVITY

What do you like to see and do on vacation? Put an X next to the things you like.

____ Sunbathe by a pool

____ Go to a theme park

____ Travel in a car

____ See a famous city

____ Go camping

____ See famous buildings

____ Go shopping

____ Stay in expensive hotels

____ Travel in a tour bus

____ See a place of natural beauty

Share your answers with your classmates. What do most of the students like to do on vacation?

WRITING

Write 5 sentences. Say where you like to go on vacation and the things you like to do there.

EXAMPLE:

I like to go to Florida. I like to go to the beach.

1. _____

2. _____

3. _____

4. _____

5. _____

DID YOU KNOW . . . ?

Florida grows more oranges than any other state.

UNIT 2

Washington

PREREADING

Answer the questions.

1. Which is better—a lot of rain or a lot of sun? Why?

2. What can you do in a place with mountains, rivers, and forests?

3. Why do people move to a new state?

Washington

Why is Washington different from every other state in the United States? It is the only state named after a president. Washington is named after the first president of the United States, George Washington. It is a beautiful state. People call it the "Evergreen State." Washington is very green because it rains a lot there.

The rain helps many things grow. There are trees and **forests** everywhere. People **cut down** the trees for wood. They plant a new tree for each tree that they cut down, so Washington has beautiful forests. There are also many fruit trees. Washington is number one in the United States for apples and pears.

Washington has a lot of mountains and rivers. There are 40 kinds of fish in the rivers, but Washington is most famous for its **salmon**. Washington also has a lot of **volcanoes**. In 1980 the volcano at Mount St. Helens **erupted**. The **smoke** from the mountain turned the day into night. Trees and plants died. Sixty people near Mount St. Helens died. But today new life is back on the mountain. Scientists are very surprised that animals and plants are back so soon.

There are over 4 million people in Washington. Many people go there to visit. Some like it a lot, and they decide to stay. Every year, more and more people come to live in this beautiful state.

VOCABULARY

Match the words and the pictures. Write your answer on the line.

forests	salmon	~~erupted~~
cut down	volcanoes	smoke

1. ___erupted___

2. _____

3. _____

4. _____

5. _____

6. _____

COMPREHENSION

 UNDERSTANDING THE MAIN IDEA

Circle the letter of the best answer.

1. Washington is ____.

    a. where George Washington's family lives

    b. a very green state

    c. the state where the president lives

2. Washington has ____.

    a. a lot of forests, mountains, and rivers

    b. one volcano

    c. no fruit trees

Circle *T* if the sentence is true. Circle *F* if the sentence is false.

1. There are many states named after a U.S. president.   T   Ⓕ
2. There are not many trees in Washington.   T   F
3. Washington is famous for its oranges.   T   F
4. Mount St. Helens erupted in 1990.   T   F
5. Sixty people died when the volcano erupted.   T   F

ACTIVITY

Which outdoor sports do you like? Talk with a partner.

skiing	rock climbing	rafting	hiking
bicycling	camping	fishing	swimming

Share your answers with your classmates. Which sport do people like most? Least? Why?

WRITING

Imagine you are lost in a forest. Write a sentence to answer each question.

1. What do you eat?

   I eat plants. _____

2. What do you drink?

   _____

3. Where do you sleep?

   _____

4. What animals do you see?

_____

5. How do you get home?

_____

6. How do you feel?

_____

DID YOU KNOW . . . ?
Bill Gates, one of the richest people in the world, lives in Washington.

UNIT 3

Vermont

PREREADING

Answer the questions.

1. What activities can you do on or around lakes?
2. What activities can you do on or around mountains?

Vermont

The word *Vermont* in French means "green mountain." In the middle of the state there are mountains. They are called the Green Mountains. There are hundreds of **lakes** in the Green Mountains. The Green Mountains are beautiful.

Forests cover most of the state. In the fall, the leaves on the trees change color. People come from everywhere to look at the beautiful colors. In the winter, the snow covers the mountains. People come to ski on the mountains.

Vermont is also famous for maple **syrup**. Americans love to eat **pancakes** with maple syrup. Maple syrup comes from maple trees. People make holes in the trees, and a sweet liquid comes out. The sweet liquid goes into **buckets**. Then people cook the liquid to make syrup. It takes about 40 gallons of sweet liquid from the maple tree to make **a gallon** of maple syrup. There are a lot of maple trees in Vermont. In fact, Vermont makes the most maple syrup in the United States.

Vermont has some unusual bridges. These bridges are not open—they are covered. There are more than 100 of these bridges, and one of them is 450 feet long. It is the longest covered bridge in the country.

The people of Vermont love the natural beauty of their state. They live a **quiet** life and enjoy nature.

VOCABULARY

Write the correct word on the line.

lakes	pancakes	a gallon
syrup	buckets	~~quiet~~

1. The people of Vermont enjoy nature. They like a _____*quiet*_____ life.

2. The mountains have _____, or large pieces of water with land around them.

3. Americans love to eat thin, soft cakes they make in a frying pan. They usually eat _____ on Sundays.

4. Americans eat pancakes with maple _____.

5. People put liquid in big containers or _____.

6. _____is a measurement for liquid. It is 4 quarts or 8 pints.

COMPREHENSION

⭐ UNDERSTANDING THE MAIN IDEA

Circle the letter of the best answer.

1. Most of Vermont has ____.

   a. mountains

   b. forests

   c. lakes

2. Vermont is famous for its ____.

   a. pancakes

   b. snow

   c. maple syrup

⭐ LOOKING FOR DETAILS

Circle *T* if the sentence is true. Circle *F* if the sentence is false.

1. The mountains are in the middle of the state.   (T)   F

2. In the winter, the leaves change color.   T   F

3. In the fall, people come to see the colors of the leaves.   T   F

4. Forty gallons of maple liquid from the tree makes
   one gallon of maple syrup.   T   F

5. Vermont has the longest covered bridge.   T   F

ACTIVITY

Think of the best places to live. Talk about them with a partner. Use some of these words.

trees	rivers	mountains with snow	few people
lakes	by the sea	a lot of people	sandy beaches

Share your answers with your classmates. What kinds of places do people like most? Least? Why?

WRITING

Write 5 sentences about the most perfect place you can think of.

EXAMPLE:

I love Costa Rica. There are a lot of trees and lakes. It has the best beaches.

1. _____
2. _____
3. _____
4. _____
5. _____

DID YOU KNOW . . . ?
There are no McDonald's in Montpelier, the state capital of Vermont.

PART 2

U.S. INVENTIONS AND INVENTORS

Unit 4 Spencer's Microwave Oven
Unit 5 Josephine Cochrane's Dishwasher
Unit 6 Patricia Bath's Laser

INVENTIONS THAT ENTERTAIN US

Phonograph (1877)

Thomas Edison invented the phonograph.

Television (1924)

Vladimir Zworykin invented the television.

INVENTIONS THAT MAKE LIFE EASIER

Dishwasher (1886)

Josephine Cochrane invented the dishwasher.

Microwave Oven (1945)

Percy Spencer invented the microwave oven.

INVENTIONS THAT TAKE US FROM PLACE TO PLACE

Motor Airplane (1903)

Orville and Wilbur Wright flew in their motor airplane.

Helicopter (1939)

Igor Sikorsky built the helicopter.

INVENTIONS THAT HELP OUR HEALTH

Polio Vaccine (1955)

Jonas Salk developed the polio vaccine.

Laser for Cataracts (1986)

Patricia Bath invented the laser for cataracts of the eye.

INVENTIONS THAT HELP US COMMUNICATE

Telephone (1876)

Alexander Graham Bell invented the telephone.

Xerox Machine (1938)

Chester Carlson invented the Xerox machine to make copies.

OTHER IMPORTANT INVENTIONS AND INVENTORS

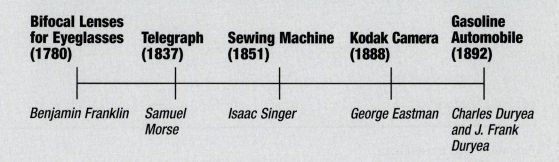

Bifocal Lenses for Eyeglasses (1780)	Telegraph (1837)	Sewing Machine (1851)	Kodak Camera (1888)	Gasoline Automobile (1892)
Benjamin Franklin	Samuel Morse	Isaac Singer	George Eastman	Charles Duryea and J. Frank Duryea

To quiz yourself about **U.S. INVENTIONS AND INVENTORS,** *go to page 112.*

UNIT 4

Spencer's Microwave Oven

PREREADING

Answer the questions.

1. Is a microwave oven useful? Why?
2. What can you do with a microwave oven?
3. What can't you do well in with a microwave oven?

Spencer's Microwave Oven

During World War II, the British used microwaves to find enemy airplanes. At that time, Percy Spencer was an engineer for the Raytheon Company in the United States. His job was to make magnetrons, machines that make microwaves. He sent these machines to the British.

The invention of the microwave oven was an accident. One day, Spencer stopped in front of a magnetron. At that moment he **noticed** something. The chocolate bar in his pocket **melted**. He didn't understand this. He tried something else. He put popcorn next to the magnetron. This time the popcorn **popped** everywhere in the laboratory. The next morning, Spencer and another engineer put an egg near the magnetron. After a few seconds, the egg **exploded** in the other engineer's face. Spencer had an idea. He thought it was possible to cook other foods quickly in this way.

The Raytheon Company worked on Spencer's idea. In 1947, Raytheon made a microwave oven. The oven was 5½ feet tall and **weighed** 750 pounds. The first microwave ovens were good only for very large kitchens in restaurants. Cooks noticed the ovens weren't good for all kinds of food. Meat wasn't brown on top. French fries were white and soft.

Over the years, microwave ovens **became** smaller and better for homes. Today, two out of three homes in the United States have microwave ovens.

VOCABULARY

Write the correct word on the line.

| noticed | ~~popped~~ | weighed |
| melted | exploded | became |

1. When the popcorn was hot, it made a loud noise like "pop." The popcorn _____**popped**_____.

2. Microwave ovens changed. They were big but are smaller now. They _____ smaller.

3. When the chocolate bar was hot, it became a liquid. The chocolate _____.

4. Spencer looked and saw his chocolate was different. He _____ it.

5. The egg was very hot. Then there was a "bang!" like a bomb. The egg was on the engineer's face. It _____.

6. The first microwave was very heavy. It _____ 750 pounds.

COMPREHENSION

⭐ UNDERSTANDING THE MAIN IDEA

Circle the letter of the best answer.

1. The invention of the microwave oven _____.
   a. helped the British
   b. was an accident
   c. was not an accident

2. The first microwave ovens were _____.
   a. very big
   b. for meat and French fries
   c. for homes

LOOKING FOR DETAILS

One word in each sentence is *not* correct. Cross out the word and write the correct answer above it.

1. The British used microwaves to ~~make~~ *find* airplanes.

2. The chocolate bar in his pocket popped.

3. The first microwave oven weighed 750 tons.

4. French fries were brown and soft.

5. Two out four homes in the United States today have microwave ovens.

ACTIVITY

Think about these inventions. Are they good or bad? Why?

cell phone with camera	digital camera	microwave oven
computer games	dishwasher	robots

Talk with a partner. Which inventions does your partner think are good? Which does your partner think are bad? Why?

WRITING

Look at the pictures. Make sentences with the words under the pictures. Write your sentences on the lines.

1. Spencer / be / an engineer / Raytheon Company

2. One day, Spencer / stop / magnetron

3. The chocolate bar / pocket / melt

4. Spencer / put / popcorn / magnetron

5. Popcorn / pop / laboratory

6. Spencer / have / an idea

1. _Spencer was an engineer for the Raytheon Company._

2. _____

3. _____

4. _____

5. _____

6. _____

DID YOU KNOW . . . ?
Percy Spencer invented more than 150 things, but he didn't have a high school education!

Josephine Cochrane's Dishwasher

PREREADING

Answer the questions.

1. What do you put in a dishwasher?
2. Why do people use dishwashers?
3. Do you use a dishwasher, or do you wash dishes by hand? Which do you like better?

Josephine Cochrane's Dishwasher

Josephine Cochrane was a very rich woman. She had many beautiful things. She never washed dishes or did housework. She had **servants** to do the work for her. Mrs. Cochrane had a very good life. But Mrs. Cochrane was not happy! Why? Her servants always **broke** her **lovely** dishes. One day another dish broke. Mrs. Cochrane got angry. She decided to do something. She decided to make a machine that washed dishes.

Mrs. Cochrane did not know anything about machines, so she asked her friends for help. Finally, she made a dishwasher. It had places for plates, **saucers**, and cups. It was a lot like dishwashers today. She made the machine and showed it to her friends. Her friends thought the machine was **amazing**. They told other friends. Soon many people knew about Mrs. Cochrane's machine. Restaurants and hotels wanted to have a machine. It was 1886. Mrs. Cochrane started a **company** to make dishwashers.

Later, her company made the first dishwashers for the home. She named her dishwasher Kitchen-Aid. Today, half the homes in the United States have dishwashers. Many people still buy Kitchen-Aid dishwashers. Everyone can thank Mrs. Cochrane for saving their nice dishes.

VOCABULARY

Write the correct word on the line.

servants	lovely	~~amazing~~
broke	saucers	company

1. Mrs. Cochrane's friends saw her dishwasher. They were very surprised.
   They thought it was ____amazing____.

2. Mrs. Cochrane liked to have tea parties. She wanted to serve her tea in
   beautiful cups and _____.

3. Josephine Cochrane started her own _____. The people
   who worked there made dishwashers.

4. Mrs. Cochrane had _____ to do all her housework for her.

5. Mrs. Cochrane's dishes were very pretty. She told the servants to be
   careful with her _____ dishes.

6. Sometimes the servants dropped Mrs. Cochrane's dishes and
   they _____.

COMPREHENSION

⭐ FOLLOWING THE SEQUENCE

**What happened first? Write *1* on the line. What happened next? Write
2 on the line.**

1. _2_ Mrs. Cochrane decided to make a dishwashing machine.

   _1_ Mrs. Cochrane's servants broke her dishes.

2. ___ Mrs. Cochrane made a dishwasher.

   ___ Mrs. Cochrane asked her friends for help.

3. ___ Mrs. Cochrane's friends thought the machine was amazing.

   ___ Mrs. Cochrane showed the machine to her friends.

4. ＿＿＿ Restaurants and hotels wanted to have Mrs. Cochrane's dishwasher.

＿＿＿ Mrs. Cochrane's friends talked to people about the machine.

5. ＿＿＿ Mrs. Cochrane started a company.

＿＿＿ Mrs. Cochrane's company made dishwashers for the home.

⭐ LOOKING FOR DETAILS

Which sentence is correct? Circle *a* or *b*.

1. a. Mrs. Cochrane never washed dishes.

   b. Mrs. Cochrane always washed dishes.

2. a. Mrs. Cochrane's friends made a dishwasher.

   b. Mrs. Cochrane made a dishwasher.

3. a. Mrs. Cochrane showed the machine to her friends.

   b. Mrs. Cochrane showed the machine to hotels.

4. a. She named her dishwasher Kitchen-Aid.

   b. Her friends named her dishwasher Kitchen-Aid.

5. a. Today, half the homes in the United States have dishwashers.

   b. Today, two out of three homes in the United States have dishwashers.

ACTIVITY

Talk with a partner. What machines do you use? What machines do you want?

EXAMPLE:

I use a vacuum cleaner. I want a dishwasher.

dishwasher	microwave oven	washing machine
vacuum cleaner	toaster	

Share your answers with your classmates. What machines do people use the most? What machines do people want the most?

WRITING

Look at the pictures. Make sentences with the words under the pictures. Write your sentences on the lines.

1. Mrs. Cochrane / have / beautiful things

2. Mrs.Cochrane / never do / housework

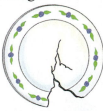

3. Mrs. Cochrane's servants / broke / dishes

4. Mrs. Cochrane / got / angry

5. Mrs. Cochrane / made / dishwasher

6. Mrs. Cochrane / started / company

1. *Mrs. Cochrane had many beautiful things.* _____

2. _____

3. _____

4. _____

5. _____

6. _____

DID YOU KNOW . . . ?

An automatic dishwasher uses approximately 9 to 12 gallons of water. Hand-washing dishes can use up to 20 gallons.

Patricia Bath's Laser

Dr. Patricia Bath

PREREADING

Answer the questions.

1. What eye problems do people have?
2. What are some ways to help these problems?

Patricia Bath's Laser

Do you know somebody with a **cataract**? As people get older, they can get cataracts in the eye. People cannot see clearly with a cataract. Some people cannot see at all. There was surgery, or a medical operation, to **remove** some cataracts. The surgery wasn't easy. Sometimes it was **painful**.

An African-American woman changed all this. Her name is Dr. Patricia Bath. In 1986, Dr. Bath invented a new laser[1] for surgery. She changed cataract surgery. It is now **accurate**, easy, and not painful. Dr. Bath helped many people. They were blind for many years. Now they can see.

Dr. Patricia Bath is a world-famous eye doctor and eye **surgeon**. The most important thing for Dr. Bath is to help people who cannot see. She is one of the people who started the American Institute for the Prevention of Blindness (AIPB). This organization wants to give eye care to all people, everywhere. Dr. Bath is director of the AIPB. She gives her own money to this. She also gets companies to give free **equipment** for eye surgery. She travels around the world. She teaches new methods and does eye surgery for free. Famous universities have programs to train students to work for the institute.

What does she want most in life? She wants to stop blindness around the world.

[1]*laser:* a machine that uses energy and light

VOCABULARY

Write the correct word on the line.

| cataract | painful | ~~surgeon~~ |
| remove | accurate | equipment |

1. A doctor who does operations is a _____*surgeon*_____.
2. A _____ is a problem in the eye.
3. Now it is possible to take out or _____ cataracts.
4. In the old days, the surgery was _____ —it hurt.
5. Today, the laser is exact and careful. It is _____.
6. The AIPB gets free _____, or tools, from manufacturers.

COMPREHENSION

UNDERSTANDING THE MAIN IDEA

Circle the letter of the best answer.

1. Patricia Bath invented ____.

    a. cataracts

    b. a laser for cataracts

    c. surgery for cataracts

2. The American Institute for the Prevention of Blindness ____.

    a. is a program at famous universities

    b. gives money for equipment

    c. gives eye care to everyone

LOOKING FOR DETAILS

One word in each sentence is *not* correct. Cross out the word and write the correct answer above it.

1. Older people can get ~~blindness~~ *cataracts* in the eye.

2. Cataract surgery is now accurate, free, and not painful.

3. Dr. Bath teaches new methods and does eye surgery for students.

4. This organization wants to give eye surgery to all people, everywhere.

5. Dr. Patricia Bath wants to stop cataracts around the world.

ACTIVITY

**Which inventions are the best in their group? Put a check mark (✔).
Then ask a classmate (for example: *Do you think the dishwasher is
the best invention?*) Which of your answers are the same?**

INVENTION	YOU	YOUR CLASSMATE
Inventions that make life easier		
Dishwasher		
Microwave		
Other		
Inventions that take us from place to place		
Jumbo jet		
Electric car		
Other		
Inventions that help our health		
The artificial heart		
Cataract laser		
Other		
Inventions that help us communicate		
Cell phone		
Computer		
Other		

WRITING

Write your answers from the Activity exercise.

EXAMPLE:

I think the dishwasher makes life easier.

1. _____

2. _____

3. _____

4. _____

DID YOU KNOW . . . ?

The human eye can see 17,000 different colors.

PART 3

U.S. ORIGINALS

Unit 7 McDonald's
Unit 8 Superman
Unit 9 Starbucks

Jeans (1860)

Levi Strauss made the first jeans.

Coca-Cola (1886)

Dr. John Pemberton was a druggist. He invented Coca-Cola in Atlanta, Georgia.

Tuxedo (1886)

Griswold Lorillard was a rich man from Tuxedo Park, New York. He wore the first tuxedo.

Peanut Butter (1890)

Dr. John Harvey Kellogg in St. Louis invented a machine to make peanut butter.

Chewing Gum (1892)

William Wrigley made flavored chewing gum.

Gillette (1903)

King Gillette made safe blades for razors.

Crossword Puzzle (1913)

Arthur Wayne published the first crossword puzzle in the newspaper.

Corn Flakes (1922)

W. W. Kellogg started the Kellogg Company. He made Corn Flakes.

Reader's Digest (1922)

Mr. and Mrs. Wallace started Reader's Digest magazine.

Superman (1939)

Jerry Siegel and Joe Shuster wrote the story of Superman.

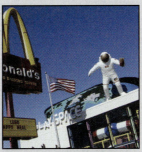

McDonald's (1961)

Two brothers sold their McDonald's restaurant for $2.5 million.

Starbucks (1971)

Three friends opened a coffee shop in Seattle, Washington.

To quiz yourself about **U.S. ORIGINALS,** *go to page 113.*

McDonald's

PREREADING

Answer the questions.

1. Why is fast food so popular?
2. What is your favorite fast food?
3. What fast-food restaurants can you name?

McDonald's

Do you have a **dream**? What do you want to do?

Maurice ("Mac") and Richard McDonald had a dream. They wanted to be movie stars. They went to California from the East coast, but they could not find jobs in the movies. They were very poor. They were **disappointed**. They had to do something to make money.

They decided to open a restaurant in San Bernardino. They wanted to try something new—a fast-food restaurant. They **borrowed** money and opened a restaurant. They called the restaurant McDonald's. Hamburgers, **milk shakes**, and French fries were on the menu. That's all. A restaurant with three things on the menu? No one thought it would work, but people loved it. The food was simple and fast. Soon, people **waited in line** outside the restaurant.

A salesman named Ray Kroc from Chicago could not understand why the restaurant needed so many milk-shake machines. He went to California to see this restaurant. He was amazed. People waited outside the restaurant to get in. He tried the food. It was great, and the restaurant was so clean.

Kroc asked the brothers to open other restaurants like this. The brothers said they made **enough** money. Kroc told the brothers they could make more money. He could open other McDonald's like this one. He would give them some money for these restaurants. The brothers agreed.

It was 1955. Kroc opened two other McDonald's, but people wanted more. Soon there were hundreds of McDonald's. The brothers had enough money. They sold McDonald's to Ray Kroc for $2.5 million dollars. Kroc became very rich. And the brothers? They were happy with their quiet life.

VOCABULARY

Write the correct word on the line.

~~dream~~	borrowed	waited in line
disappointed	milk shakes	enough

1. Mac and Richard McDonald had a _____*dream*_____. They wanted to be movie stars.

2. The McDonald brothers did not have any money to open a restaurant. They _____ money from someone.

3. Mac and Richard wanted to be movie stars, but they could not find jobs. They felt sad. They were _____.

4. Mac and Richard made a lot of _____. They used milk, ice, and sugar.

5. Mac and Richard did not need more money. They had

   _____.

6. McDonald's became a very popular restaurant. People _____ to eat there.

COMPREHENSION

⭐ **FOLLOWING THE SEQUENCE**

What happened first? Write *1* on the line. What happened next? Write *2* on the line.

1. __1__ Mac and Richard went to California. They wanted to be movie stars.

   __2__ Mac and Richard could not find jobs in the movies.

2. ____ The McDonald brothers opened a fast-food restaurant.

   ____ The McDonald brothers borrowed money.

3. ____ People waited in line to get into McDonald's.

   ____ Mac and Richard tried a simple menu—hamburgers, milk shakes, and French fries.

4. _____ Kroc thought McDonald's was a great restaurant.

    _____ Kroc went to California.

5. _____ Mac and Richard sold McDonald's to Ray Kroc for $2.5 million.

    _____ Kroc became very rich.

⭐ LOOKING FOR DETAILS

One word in each sentence is *not* correct. Cross out the word and write the correct answer above it.

1. Mac and Richard McDonald went to California from the ~~West~~ *East* coast.

2. Hamburgers, salads, and milk shakes were on the first McDonald's menu.

3. Ray Kroc was a salesman from Boston.

4. The brothers sold McDonald's to Ray Kroc for $3.5 million.

5. The brothers were unhappy with their quiet life.

ACTIVITY

Imagine you are one of the McDonald brothers. You want to sell your restaurant. Give three reasons.

> **EXAMPLE:**
>
> *I want to be rich.* _____

1. _____

2. _____

3. _____

Share your answers with your classmates. How many different reasons are there?

WRITING

Look at the pictures. Make sentences with the words under the pictures. Write your sentences on the lines.

1. Mac and Richard McDonald / opened / fast-food restaurant

2. They / call / restaurant McDonald's

3. They / have / three things on the menu

4. People / waited / line / outside / restaurant

5. Ray Kroc / went / California / see / McDonald's

6. Brothers / sold / McDonald's / Ray Kroc

1. <u>*Mac and Richard McDonald opened a fast-food restaurant.*</u>

2. _____

3. _____

4. _____

5. _____

6. _____

DID YOU KNOW . . . ?

McDonald's has a charity program. It's called The Ronald McDonald House. It helps sick children around the world.

UNIT 8

Superman

PREREADING

Answer the questions.

1. Why do so many people like Superman?
2. Do you like to read books about heroes? Do you like to see movies?
3. Who are your real-life heroes?

Superman

"Look, up in the sky. It's a bird! It's a plane! It's Superman!" Everyone knows Superman. Old people know Superman. Young people know Superman. He is famous. Millions of people buy Superman **comic books**.

The story of Superman started in 1939. Jerry Siegel and Joe Shuster were high school students. Jerry wanted to be a writer. Joe wanted to be an artist. They liked to work together. One wrote. The other drew pictures. They wrote stories with pictures for comic books.

One day, Jerry had a great new idea. It was Superman! Superman is from another **planet**, but nobody knows. He lives like an **ordinary** person. Superman does good things for people. He is a **hero**. Joe drew Superman. Joe and Jerry wanted to sell their story. They wanted to make money, but nobody bought Superman. Finally, after many years, someone wanted to buy Superman. Jerry and Joe were very excited, but they sold Superman for only a little money.

Superman became a great success. The people who owned Superman made millions of dollars. But Joe and Jerry were poor.

In 1975, Joe could not see well. He could not draw. He lived in a small apartment. Jerry worked for very little money. The two men were both old and poor. They were angry, too. They told the newspapers about their **situation**. Finally, the owners of Superman gave Joe and Jerry more money. The money helped the old men, but it was still not much. Other people made a lot more money from Superman. It was also 30 years too late. Superman is famous. His owners are rich. But Joe and Jerry were not so **lucky**.

VOCABULARY

Write the correct word on the line.

comic books	ordinary	situation
~~planet~~	hero	lucky

1. Superman was not born on Earth. He is from a different ___*planet*___.

2. The people who bought Superman became rich, but Jerry and Joe did not. They were not _____.

3. Jerry and Joe were old and poor, but others got rich from their ideas. Jerry and Joe were in a bad _____.

4. Superman helps people. He does good things for them. He is a _____.

5. Superman has a job. He does things that most people do. He lives an _____ life when he is not being a hero.

6. Jerry and Joe wrote stories with pictures when they were in high school. They liked to make _____.

COMPREHENSION

 ## UNDERSTANDING THE MAIN IDEA

Complete each sentence with the correct word or words. Write the letter of your answer on the line.

1. Jerry wanted to be a writer. Joe wanted to be an __*d*__.

2. People like Superman because ____.

3. Jerry and Joe told their story to the newspapers because ____.

4. The owners of Superman finally gave Joe and Jerry more ____.

a. he is a hero and he helps people
b. they wanted people to know about their situation
c. money
~~d.~~ artist

LOOKING FOR DETAILS

Circle *T* if the sentence is true. Circle *F* if the sentence is false.

1. Jerry and Joe worked well together.   (T)   F
2. Joe had the idea for Superman.   T   F
3. Jerry and Joe sold their Superman idea for a lot of money.   T   F
4. Jerry and Joe were angry when they sold Superman.   T   F
5. The people who owned Superman made millions of dollars.   T   F

ACTIVITY

Work with a partner. Talk about this situation: Two men rob a bank. They lock the people in a small room. There is not much air in the room. The robbers are driving away in a fast car.

1. What should Superman do?
2. How can Superman save the people and catch the robbers?
3. What can the people in the room do?

Share your answers with your classmates. What ideas are the same? What are the best ideas?

WRITING

Write 5 sentences about heroes.

EXAMPLE:

A hero saves people. _____

1. _____
2. _____
3. _____
4. _____
5. _____

DID YOU KNOW . . . ?

In the story, Superman lives in the city of Metropolis. There is a real city called Metropolis in the state of Illinois. The real Metropolis has Superman Square. There is also a 19-foot picture of Superman on a water tower.

44   UNIT 8

UNIT 9

Starbucks

PREREADING

Answer the questions.

1. Do you like coffee or tea?
2. What's your favorite coffee shop?
3. What do you like about it?

Starbucks

Starbucks is one of America's most popular coffee shops. You can usually find a Starbucks coffee shop near your home. Starbucks sells many kinds of coffee. You can buy hot or cold coffee in different **flavors** and cup sizes. The cup sizes have names like Short (extra small), Tall (small), Grande (medium), and Venti (large).

The story of Starbucks started in 1971 in Seattle, Washington. Three friends, Jerry Baldwin, Zev Siegel, and Gordon Bowker, opened a small coffee shop. They sold fresh **coffee beans**. In 1981, Howard Schultz joined the company. After **a trip** to Italy, Schultz had a new idea for Starbucks. In Italy he had his first *latte* (espresso coffee with hot milk). He noticed people going to coffee shops for coffee and friendship. He loved the idea. He wanted to do this in the United States.

He talked about his new idea to the owners of Starbucks. Baldwin was not happy about this idea. He wanted to sell only coffee beans. In 1985, Schultz decided to open his own **Italian-style** coffee shop. It was a great success.

By 1987, Starbucks was put up **for sale**. Schultz bought it for $3.8 million dollars. He **kept the name** Starbucks. It became the Starbucks we know today. Schulz wanted to open 125 Starbucks in 5 years. In 1992, there were 165 Starbucks. Everybody loved Starbucks. Today there are more than 12,000 Starbucks coffee shops around the world.

VOCABULARY

Write the correct word on the line.

flavors	a trip	~~for sale~~
coffee beans	Italian style	kept the name

1. When you want to sell something, it is ____*for sale*____ .

2. Schultz went on _____ to Italy.

3. The original name Starbucks did not change. Schultz _____ .

4. You can buy coffee with a special taste like vanilla or chocolate. These are different _____ .

5. _____ is the way Italians do it.

6. Coffee is made from the seeds of the coffee plant. These are _____ .

COMPREHENSION

⭐ FOLLOWING THE SEQUENCE

What happened first? Write *1* on the line. What happened next? Write *2* on the line.

1. __2__ Three friends sold coffee beans.

   __1__ Jerry Baldwin, Zev Siegel, and Gordon Bowker opened a coffee shop.

2. ____ Howard Schultz joined the company.

   ____ Schultz went to Italy.

3. ____ Schultz opened an Italian-style coffee shop.

   ____ He talked to Baldwin about his new idea.

4. ____ Schultz bought Starbucks.

   ____ Baldwin decided to sell Starbucks.

5. ____ There are more than 12,000 Starbucks today.

   ____ Schultz wanted to open 125 Starbucks by 1992.

One word in each sentence is *not* correct. Cross out the word and write the correct answer above it.

1. You can buy coffee in different ~~colors~~ *flavors*.

2. The story of Starbucks started in 1981 in Washington.

3. Three friends made coffee beans.

4. Baldwin wanted to sell only coffee cups.

5. Today there are more than 12,000 Starbucks around the country.

ACTIVITY

What are your classmates' favorite drinks and snacks? Fill in the chart.

NAME	FAVORITE DRINK	FAVORITE SNACK
Miguel	latte	potato chips

Share your answers with your classmates. What is the most popular drink? What is the most popular snack?

WRITING

Write about how you make tea or coffee.

EXAMPLE:

Tea with lemon _____

First, boil water. _____

_____

First, _____

Second, _____

Third, _____

Then _____

Finally, _____

DID YOU KNOW . . . ?

There is a Starbucks in The Forbidden City in Beijing, the largest palace in the world.

PART 4

HOLIDAYS AND SPECIAL DAYS

Unit 10 New Year's Celebrations
Unit 11 St. Patrick's Day
Unit 12 Labor Day

JANUARY

New Year's Day

New Year's Day is January 1. Many people watch the Rose Bowl football game on television.

Chinese New Year

Chinese-Americans celebrate the New Year in January or February.

Martin Luther King Day

On Martin Luther King Day, people remember this famous leader.

FEBRUARY

Valentine's Day

On February 14, people send cards and give flowers and chocolates to people they love.

Presidents' Day

People remember George Washington and Abraham Lincoln on the third Monday in February.

MARCH

St. Patrick's Day

On March 17, Irish-Americans remember St. Patrick. People wear green because it is the color of Ireland.

APRIL

MAY

Cinco de Mayo
Mexican-Americans celebrate this day on May 5.

Memorial Day

Americans remember people who died in U.S. wars on the last Monday in May.

JUNE

JULY

Independence Day

July 4 is the birthday of the United States.

AUGUST

SEPTEMBER

Labor Day

On the first Monday in September, people remember American workers. In 1869 workers started a labor union. Today, most people do not work on this day.

OCTOBER

Halloween

On October 31, children wear costumes. They get candy.

NOVEMBER

Veterans Day

On November 11, people remember American soldiers.

Thanksgiving

In the United States, families get together and have a big dinner on the fourth Thursday in November. They eat turkey and pumpkin pie.

DECEMBER

Christmas

On December 25, Christians celebrate Christmas.

Hanukkah

In December, Jewish people celebrate Hanukkah.

To quiz yourself about HOLIDAYS AND SPECIAL DAYS, *go to page 114.*

New Year's Celebrations

PREREADING

Answer the questions.

1. Where are the people in the picture?
2. What are they doing?
3. How do you celebrate the New Year?

New Year's Celebrations

Five, four, three, two, one! Happy New Year! It is twelve o'clock midnight. The year ends. A new one begins. Some people are happy. Some people are sad. Everyone thinks about the past year and the next year.

New Year's Eve is December 31. It is the night before New Year's Day. People like to be with friends and family. They do not want to be alone. They want to be happy. Many people go to parties or restaurants. Everyone waits for midnight. They eat, drink, and dance. At midnight, people **ring bells** and **blow horns**. People say, "Happy New Year!" They kiss and **hug**.

The biggest New Year's Eve **celebration** is in New York City. A million people go to Times Square. They wait for the new year. Famous singers sing to the **crowd**. A large ball slowly comes down from a tall building. Everyone watches it. The new year begins when the ball reaches the bottom. There is a lot of noise. People watch this on television. Many people stay awake until two or three o'clock in the morning.

January 1 is New Year's Day. It is a national holiday. People do not work. They stay at home. Many Americans watch television on New Year's Day. In the morning, they watch the Tournament of Roses Parade. Everything in the **parade** has flowers. After the parade, they watch college football games.

On New Year's Day, many Americans decide to change their bad habits. Some promise to spend less money. Some promise to eat less food. Most people forget about their promises.

VOCABULARY

Match the words and the pictures. Write your answer on the line.

ring bells	~~hug~~	crowd
blow horns	celebration	parade

1. _____hug_____   2. _____   3. _____

4. _____   5. _____   6. _____

COMPREHENSION

 UNDERSTANDING THE MAIN IDEA

Circle the letter of the best answer.

1. People want to be with friends and family on New Year's Eve because _____.

    a. there are many things to see and do on New Year's Eve

    b. they do not want to stay home and watch TV

    c. they do not want to be alone. They want to be happy

2. On New Year's Day, people watch television because _____.

    a. they like to see parades and football games

    b. they do not want to be sad

    c. they want to change their bad habits

Circle *T* if the sentence is true. Circle *F* if the sentence is false.

1. Americans like to visit new places to celebrate the new year.   T   Ⓕ
2. People like to go to bed early on New Year's Eve.   T   F
3. The biggest New Year's Eve celebration is in California.   T   F
4. Most people work on New Year's Day.   T   F
5. Many people promise to change their bad habits on New Year's Day.   T   F

ACTIVITY

Interview a partner. Ask the questions.

1. What are two good things about last year?
2. What are two bad things about last year?
3. What do you want to do next year?

Share your answers with your classmates. Who has answers like yours?

WRITING

Write 3 promises on the lines.

1. Next year I want to _____.
2. Next year I want to _____.
3. Next year I want to _____.

What is your idea of a perfect year? Write two sentences.

> **EXAMPLE:**
>
> *I spend a lot of time with my family.* _____

1. _____
2. _____

DID YOU KNOW . . . ?

The tradition of the large ball coming down in Times Square started in 1907. The original ball was wood and iron. Today the ball is Waterford Crystal and weighs 1,070 pounds!

St. Patrick's Day

PREREADING

Answer the questions.

1. What is your favorite holiday?
2. Does your holiday have a special color?
3. What do people do on your favorite holiday?

St. Patrick's Day

Many **Irish** people live in the United States. St. Patrick's Day is their holiday. St. Patrick's Day is not a national holiday in the United States. It is a special day because many people in the United States celebrate it. They remember the Irish people in the United States and Ireland.

Ireland has a lot of **green** grass, so green is the color of Ireland. Many people wear green on St. Patrick's Day. Ireland also has a lot of **shamrocks**. They are small plants with three leaves. A shamrock with four leaves brings good luck. Many people wear shamrocks on St. Patrick's Day.

St. Patrick's Day honors St. Patrick. He was a **priest** in Ireland. He helped the Irish learn about Christianity. On St. Patrick's Day, there are parades. People sing, dance, and eat Irish food. Some people make green drinks. In **Chicago**, they color the river green! Big cities with a lot of Irish people, such as New York, Boston, and Philadelphia, have huge St. Patrick's Day parades. The people in the parades wear Irish clothes. Bands play songs about Ireland.

In 1845, many people from Ireland moved to the United States. They moved because they did not have enough food. On St. Patrick's Day the Irish people in the United States remember and honor their country.

VOCABULARY

Draw a line to match the words that go together.

1. Irish   country
2. Ireland   plant
3. green   city
4. shamrock   religious person; works in a church
5. priest   nationality
6. Chicago   color

COMPREHENSION

⭐ UNDERSTANDING THE MAIN IDEA

Circle the letter of the best answer.

1. St. Patrick's Day is a ____.
   a. holiday for the color green
   b. holiday for the Irish
   c. national holiday

2. On St. Patrick's Day, people
   ____.
   a. wear green
   b. eat shamrocks
   c. wear grass

3. On St. Patricks' Day, people ____.
   a. remember the year the Irish left Ireland
   b. honor a priest
   c. celebrate only in Boston

⭐ LOOKING FOR DETAILS

Complete each sentence with the correct words. Write the letter of your answer on the line.

1. Green is the color of Ireland because Ireland __d__.
2. There are many stories ____.
3. St. Patrick is important to the Irish because ____.
4. Many Irish people moved to the United States because ____.
5. There are parades ____.

a. in cities like New York and Boston
b. he helped them learn about Christianity
c. they did not have enough food
d. has a lot of green grass
e. about St. Patrick

ACTIVITY

Ask a classmate about his or her favorite holiday. Talk about a holiday in the United States or another country. Find the answers to the questions.

1. What is the name of your favorite holiday?
2. When do people celebrate the holiday?
3. What do people wear?
4. What do people do?
5. Why is the holiday special?

Share your partner's answers with your classmates. Write the names of everyone's holiday on the board. Which holiday is the most fun? Which holiday is the most interesting?

WRITING

Write 5 sentences about a special holiday in the United States or another country.

EXAMPLE:

Thanksgiving is a special holiday. Families get together and eat a large meal.

1. _____
2. _____
3. _____
4. _____
5. _____

 DID YOU KNOW . . . ?
Green is the color of St. Patrick's day because it's the color of grass.

Labor Day

PREREADING

Answer the questions.

1. What are the people in the picture doing?
2. What year do you think it is?
3. What are some holidays that you know for workers?

Labor Day

In the 1800s, men and women worked 12 to 16 hours a day. They worked 7 days a week. They made very little money. Workers had no **benefits**. They did not get any money when they were sick. They did not get vacations. Children worked, too. Women and children worked for very little money in the **factories**. One of these children was Peter McGuire. In 1863, he was 11 years old, and he worked in a factory.

The workers wanted a better life, but they were afraid to ask for better pay. They did not want to **lose** their jobs. But when workers came together, they were not afraid. When they all asked for benefits, it was easier. Finally, workers came together in **labor unions**.

The first labor union started in 1869. The unions helped workers **improve** their lives. Peter McGuire became president of a labor union. He wanted a holiday for workers. His dream came true on September 5, 1882. There was a big parade in New York City for all the workers in the United States. In 1894, Labor Day became a national holiday.

Now Labor Day is always the first Monday in September. Most people do not go to work on this day. They have a three-day weekend. Some people go to the beach. Others have a **barbecue** or a picnic or watch the Labor Day parades.

VOCABULARY

Write the correct word on the line.

benefits	lose	~~improve~~
factories	labor unions	barbecue

1. In the 1800s, workers wanted to make their lives better. They wanted to ____*improve*____ their lives.

2. Workers were afraid to ask for more money because they would _____ their jobs and not have any work.

3. Today's workers get money when they are sick. They get vacations. These are examples of _____.

4. In the 1800s, women and children worked in _____. They made clothes, shoes, and many other things there.

5. On Labor Day, many people have a _____ outdoors. They cook chicken, hamburgers, or hotdogs over a fire.

6. Workers finally came together in groups called _____.

COMPREHENSION

⭐ **FOLLOWING THE SEQUENCE**

What happened first? Write *1* on the line. What happened next? Write *2* on the line.

1. __1__ Men and women worked 14 hours a day 7 days a week.

   __2__ Peter McGuire worked in a factory. He was 11 years old.

2. ____ Workers decided to work together.

   ____ Workers wanted to improve their lives.

3. ____ In 1869, workers came together in labor unions.

   ____ Peter McGuire became president of a labor union.

4. ____ There was a big parade in New York City for all the workers.

   ____ Peter McGuire wanted a holiday for workers.

LOOKING FOR DETAILS

Circle _T_ if the sentence is true. Circle _F_ if the sentence is false.

1. Before labor unions, workers had no vacations.   (T)   F

2. Before labor unions, women and children
   made a lot of money.   T   F

3. In the early 1800s, workers were very happy.   T   F

4. Labor unions helped workers improve their lives.   T   F

5. Peter McGuire became president of a labor union.   T   F

ACTIVITY

Work with a partner. Think about the perfect job. Answer the questions.

1. What is the job? Where is it?   3. What are your benefits?

2. How many days do you work?   4. How much do you earn?

Share your answers with your classmates. What are some of the most popular jobs? How much money do people want to earn?

WRITING

Write 3 sentences about the job that you have or want.

EXAMPLE:

I am a clerk in a shoe store. I work five nights every week. I start work at 5:30 and leave at 10:00. I like my job because it is close to home. I can walk to work. I also like to meet people.

1. _____

2. _____

3. _____

DID YOU KNOW . . . ?

Labor Day is not a holiday just in the United States. People observe Labor Day in Canada, Europe, and other industrialized countries.

PART 5

WASHINGTON, D.C.

Unit 13 The Capitol
Unit 14 The Smithsonian Institution
Unit 15 Arlington National Cemetery

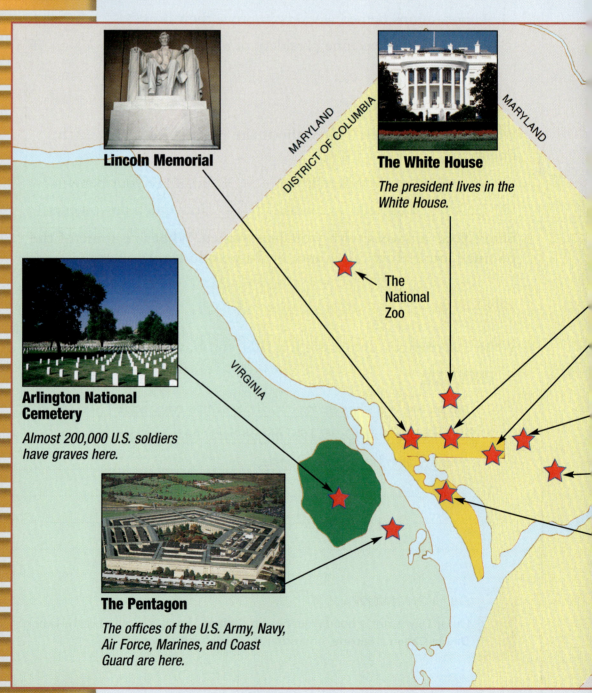

Lincoln Memorial

The White House

The president lives in the White House.

The National Zoo

Arlington National Cemetery

Almost 200,000 U.S. soldiers have graves here.

The Pentagon

The offices of the U.S. Army, Navy, Air Force, Marines, and Coast Guard are here.

MARYLAND

DISTRICT OF COLUMBIA

MARYLAND

VIRGINIA

Washington Monument

The Smithsonian Institution

This is the largest museum in the world.

The Capitol Building

Congress meets in the Capitol and makes laws for the country.

The Library of Congress

The Library of Congress is the national library of the United States. It is the largest library in the world.

Jefferson Memorial

The Stars and Stripes

The red, white, and blue of the U. S. flag is sometimes called "The Stars and Stripes."

FACTS ABOUT WASHINGTON, D.C.

Washington, D.C., is the capital city. It is not a state. It is a district. The district is called the District of Columbia (D.C.).

1791 George Washington chose the place for the capital city.

1814 The British burned the White House, the Capitol, and other buildings.

1815 The Americans rebuilt the White House, the Capitol, and other buildings.

1912 Japan gave the United States 3,000 cherry trees.

1963 Over 200,000 people came to Washington, D.C. Martin Luther King gave his famous speech, "I Have a Dream."

Today about 550,000 people live in Washington, D.C.

To quiz yourself about WASHINGTON, D.C, *go to page 115.*

The Capitol

PREREADING

Answer the questions.

1. Think of another country. Who tells people what they can and cannot do?
2. Where do people in the government work?
3. What do you know about government in the United States?

The Capitol

The United States Congress works in the Capitol building in Washington, D.C. In the Capitol, **members** of Congress **pass laws** for the country. Congress has two parts. One is the Senate. The other is the House of Representatives. People in each state **elect** members of Congress. Visitors can watch members of Congress work on laws. There is a **statue** on top of the Capitol. It is the goddess of Freedom. When Congress meets, the statue has a light.

Today, the Capitol has 540 rooms. It has restaurants, kitchens, post offices, a **barbershop**, and a prayer room. Visitors can see many of these rooms. They can also see hundreds of paintings and works of art in the Capitol.

The members of the House of Representatives and the Senate have offices in another building. Underground trains go from the office building to the Capitol. Senators and congressmen have people who work for them. Sometimes these **staff** members stay in the Capitol building. They call the congressmen and congresswomen when something important happens. The congressmen and congresswomen come quickly on the train. They get there in time to vote. But this train is not just for members of Congress. Visitors can take this train, too.

VOCABULARY

Write the correct word on the line.

~~members~~	elect	barbershop
pass laws	statue	staff

1. The congressmen and congresswomen are part of Congress. They are
   _____members_____ of Congress.

2. People who work for a senator are part of the senator's _____.

3. A _____ is a place where men go to get their hair cut.

4. People vote to choose members of the Senate and House of
   Representatives. They _____ them to Congress.

5. The _____ on top of the Capitol building is the goddess of
   Freedom. It is a woman made of stone.

6. Congress decides what citizens can and cannot do. Members of
   Congress _____.

COMPREHENSION

⭐ UNDERSTANDING THE MAIN IDEA

**Complete each sentence with the correct words. Write the letter of
your answer on the line.**

1. The Capitol building is in __c__.
2. The members of Congress have
   very important work. They ____.
3. The people of each state
   elect ____.
4. Staff members sometimes stay
   in the Capitol. They call the
   congressmen and congresswomen when ____.

a. members of Congress
b. something important happens
~~c.~~ Washington, D.C.
d. make laws for the country

⭐ LOOKING FOR DETAILS

Circle *T* if the sentence is true. Circle *F* if the sentence is false.

1. The Capitol is divided into two parts. They are   T   (F)
   the Senate and the House of Representatives.
2. When Congress meets, there is a flag on   T   F
   top of the Capitol.
3. The Capitol has post offices and restaurants.   T   F
4. Visitors can see some of the rooms   T   F
   in the Capitol.
5. Visitors cannot watch the members of Congress.   T   F

ACTIVITY

Work in a small group. Read these old laws. Are they good or bad?

1. Everybody must take a bath at least once a year.
2. You cannot travel on a bus if you eat garlic.
3. Teachers can hit students.
4. All businesses must close on Sunday.

Share your answers with your classmates. Which laws do people think are good? Which do they think are bad? Why?

WRITING

Imagine you are a member of Congress. Write 2 new laws. Share your laws with your classmates.

> **EXAMPLE:**
>
> *People cannot smoke in restaurants.*

1. _____

2. _____

DID YOU KNOW . . . ?

A donkey represents the Democratic Party, and an elephant represents the Republican Party.

UNIT 14

The Smithsonian Institution

PREREADING

Answer the questions.

1. Why are museums important?
2. What museums do you know?
3. What do you like to see in a museum?

The Smithsonian Institution

People do unusual things with their money. Some people die and give all their money to their pets. Other people give their money to people they do not know. One rich man, James Smithson, gave everything to a country—the United States.

In the 1800s, James Smithson was a rich British **scientist**. He never visited the United States. He had no friends there. But he died and gave all his money to the United States. No one knows why he **selected** this country. But they knew one thing—Smithson wanted his money to start a place where people could learn. The first building of the Smithsonian Institution opened in Washington, D.C., in 1846. Little by little, the Smithsonian grew.

Today, the Smithsonian Institution is the largest museum in the world. The Smithsonian has many **galleries** and 13 museums. The National Zoo is there, too. You can learn many interesting things at the Smithsonian. You can learn about American history, art, and technology. At the National History Museum, you can see the first Star Spangled Banner. This is another name for the **flag** of the United States. At the National Air and Space Museum, you can see the first airplane built by the Wright Brothers in 1903. The Smithsonian is the world's most **popular** museum. About 8 million people go there every year. The Smithsonian has about 140 million **objects**. It can take you 265 years to see everything!

VOCABULARY

Write the correct word on the line.

~~scientist~~	galleries	popular
selected	flag	objects

1. A person who studies plants, animals, and other things is a

   _____ *scientist* _____.

2. There are many _____ in the Smithsonian. In fact, there
   are 140 million things to see.

3. America's _____ is red, white, and blue.

4. Smithson gave his money to the United States. No one knows why
   he _____ the United States.

5. The Smithsonian has many works of art. You can see them in
   the _____.

6. Many people like the Smithsonian. It is very _____.

COMPREHENSION

⭐ FOLLOWING THE SEQUENCE

**What happened first? Write *1* on the line. What happened next? Write
2 on the line.**

1. __2__ The United States built the Smithsonian Institution.

   __1__ James Smithson gave his money to the United States.

2. ____ The Smithsonian is the most popular museum.

   ____ The Smithsonian opened in 1846.

3. ____ The first airplane flies.

   ____ The first airplane is in the National Air and Space Museum.

4. ____ You can learn many interesting things at the Smithsonian.

   ____ James Smithson wanted to build a place where people could learn.

5. ____ The Smithsonian was one building in 1846.

   ____ The Smithsonian has many galleries and 13 museums.

⭐ LOOKING FOR DETAILS

Complete each sentence with the correct words. Write the letter of your answer on the line.

1. The Smithsonian Institution is the largest __c__ .
2. Smithson wanted to build a place where people can ____ .
3. The Smithsonian Institution has ____ .
4. At the National Air and Space Museum, you can see the ____ .
5. It can take over 200 years to see everything because ____ .

a. learn many things
b. there are about 140 million objects in the Smithsonian
c. museum in the world
d. 13 museums
e. first airplane

ACTIVITY

Work with a partner. Look at the pictures and the words that go with them. Imagine you work at a museum. You take people to see the museum. How can you solve each problem?

1. You go to the hotel to pick up the people. One man is not there.

2. The bus breaks down on the way.

3. At the museum, two people talk during the lecture.

4. A baby cries. He does not stop crying.

Share your answers with your classmates. Are any of your answers the same?

WRITING

Imagine you are very rich. You do not have a family. Who or what do you give your money to? Why? Write 5 sentences.

I want to give my money to _____

because _____

_____

_____

_____

_____

DID YOU KNOW . . . ?

James Smithson's bones are in the Smithsonian Castle, one of the buildings of the Smithsonian Institution.

Arlington National Cemetery

PREREADING

Answer the questions.

1. Do you like to visit famous places? Why?
2. Do most cemeteries look like the one in the picture? If not, what is different?
3. Think of another country. Where are famous people buried?

Arlington National Cemetery

People usually do not like to visit cemeteries. Most of us never want to go to a cemetery! But some cemeteries have thousands of visitors every year. These cemeteries have important people's graves. There are special **monuments** and statues and interesting things to read. Arlington National Cemetery is interesting and very beautiful.

Arlington National Cemetery is near Washington, D.C. It is in a beautiful part of Virginia. There are many trees and lots of green grass. Almost 2,000 American soldiers have graves there. The graves of presidents and other important people are also in the cemetery. You can see the grave of President John F. Kennedy. It has a **flame** that burns all the time. The grave of his brother, Senator Robert F. Kennedy, is nearby. You can also see a tomb for the **astronauts** who died in the **space shuttle** *Challenger*.

The famous **Tomb** of the Unknown Soldier is in Arlington National Cemetery. It has the bodies of three United States soldiers. No one knows who they are. This tomb is for all the U.S. soldiers who die in wars. There is a **guard** in front of the tomb. He walks up and down in front of the tomb 42 times each hour. Every hour during the day, a new guard comes. At night, a new guard comes every two hours. Thousands of people come to see the "changing of the guard."

VOCABULARY

Match the words and the pictures. Write your answer on the line.

monument	astronaut	tomb
flame	~~space shuttle~~	guard

1. _space shuttle_

2. _____

3. _____

4. _____

5. _____

6. _____

⭐ COMPREHENSION

UNDERSTANDING THE MAIN IDEA

Circle the letter of the best answer.

1. Many people visit Arlington National Cemetery because ____.
   a. they like to see the trees
   b. they want to meet special people in the United States
   c. they want to see an important and interesting place

2. Arlington National Cemetery has the graves of ____.
   a. presidents only
   b. soldiers only
   c. soldiers and important people

3. The Tomb of the Unknown Soldier is important because ____.

    a. people can watch the changing of the guard there

    b. it is for all the soldiers who die for America

    c. it has the body of a very famous American

 LOOKING FOR DETAILS

One word in each sentence is *not* correct. Cross out the word and write the correct answer above it.

1. Arlington National Cemetery is near ~~Virginia~~ *Washington*.

2. Arlington National Cemetery has the graves of almost 5,000 American soldiers.

3. There is a statue on the grave of President John F. Kennedy.

4. The cemetery has a tomb for the soldiers who died in the space shuttle *Challenger*.

5. A president walks up and down in front of the Tomb of the Unknown Soldier.

ACTIVITY

Write the names of the places you want to visit. Write the names of the places you do not want to visit.

the White House	the Pentagon	the Statue of Liberty
Mount Rushmore	the Liberty Bell	Yellowstone National Park

1. I want to go to _____.

2. I do not want to go to _____.

Share your answers with your classmates. Which place is the most popular? Which is the most unpopular? Why?

WRITING

Write 5 sentences about a monument or important place in another country. What is its name? Where is it? What is it for? Why is it important?

EXAMPLE:

The Parthenon is an important place. It is in Athens, Greece.

1. _____

2. _____

3. _____

4. _____

5. _____

DID YOU KNOW . . . ?

The only two presidents buried in Arlington National Cemetery are William Howard Taft and John F. Kennedy

PART 6

U.S. ARTS AND ENTERTAINMENT

Unit 16 Walt Disney
Unit 17 Maya Lin
Unit 18 Ella Fitzgerald

ARTISTS

Maya Lin

Maya Lin is an architect. She is famous for the Vietnam Veterans' Memorial in Washington, D.C.

Red Cube, 1968

Isamu Noguchi

Isamu Noguchi's sculptures are very modern.

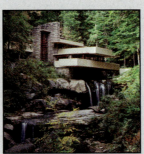

Frank Lloyd Wright

Frank Lloyd Wright was an architect. He became famous for his beautiful, unusual buildings.

Black and Purple Petunias, 1925

Georgia O'Keeffe

Georgia O'Keeffe's paintings are of flowers and modern landscapes.

WRITERS

Emily Dickinson

Emily Dickinson was a poet. She almost always stayed at home alone.

Langston Hughes

Langston Hughes was famous for his poems.

Maya Angelou

Maya Angelou is a modern writer. She writes about her childhood.

Mark Twain

Mark Twain's books are about life on the river.

PEOPLE IN ENTERTAINMENT

Ella Fitzgerald

People called Ella Fitzgerald the "First Lady of Song."

Steven Spielberg

Steven Spielberg is a movie director. He made the famous movie ET.

Walt Disney

Walt Disney was famous for his cartoons and Disneyland.

Louis Armstrong

Louis Armstrong was the first jazz trumpet player to be famous around the world.

To quiz yourself about U.S. ARTS AND ENTERTAINMENT, *go to page 116.*

Walt Disney

PREREADING

Answer the questions.

1. What are some famous Walt Disney characters?
2. What are some Walt Disney films?
3. What do you know about Disneyland?

Walt Disney

Walt Disney **grew up** on a farm. He loved to **draw** animals. Later, he wanted to get a job as a **cartoonist** for a newspaper. He was not successful. Then he got a job to make cartoons for movies. This was a new business at that time. Disney liked this idea. Hollywood was a better place for this new business.

Walt Disney moved to Hollywood. He started his own movie company in 1923. In 1928 he made his first movie about Mickey Mouse. It was a big success. Then he made a movie about Donald Duck.

Walt Disney continued to make long cartoon movies like *Snow White and the Seven Dwarfs*, *Bambi*, and *Sleeping Beauty*. His movie company was the biggest maker of cartoons in the world. Later, he made children's movies like *Mary Poppins* with real **actors**.

In 1954, Disney started to build Disneyland in California. In the first two months, over a million people came to Disneyland. It was a **huge** success. Disney planned to open a larger Disney park in Florida. He didn't see it open. He died in 1966. Walt Disney World opened in Florida in 1971.

Today, there are Disney parks in Tokyo, Japan, and outside Paris, France. People all over the world enjoy Walt Disney's **characters** and stories.

VOCABULARY

Write the correct word on the line.

~~grew up~~	cartoonist	huge
draw	actors	characters

1. Walt Disney lived on a farm from the time he was a child until he was an adult. He _____grew up_____ on a farm.

2. People love the _____ in Walt Disney's movies.

3. Walt Disney liked to make pictures, or _____ animals with a pencil or a pen.

4. Walt Disney wanted to make funny pictures for a newspaper. He wanted to be a _____.

5. The people in Disney's later movies, like *Mary Poppins*, are _____.

6. Disneyland was a very big, or _____, success.

COMPREHENSION

⭐ FOLLOWING THE SEQUENCE

What happened first? Write *1* on the line. What happened next? Write *2* on the line.

1. __1__ Disney wanted to get a job as a cartoonist for a newspaper.

   __2__ Disney got a job to make cartoons for movies.

2. ____ He started his own movie company in 1923.

   ____ He moved to Hollywood.

3. ____ He made children's movies with real actors.

   ____ He made long cartoon movies.

4. ____ Disney built Disneyland in California.

   ____ Disney built Disney World in Florida.

5. ____ Disney World in Florida opened.

   ____ Walt Disney died.

 ## LOOKING FOR DETAILS

***One* word in each sentence is *not* correct. Cross out the word and write the correct answer above it.**

1. Disney wanted to get a job as a ~~producer~~ *cartoonist* for a newspaper.

2. He started his own newspaper company in 1923.

3. Disney made children's movies with real cartoons.

4. Disneyland in California was a huge movie.

5. People all over the world enjoy Walt Disney's actors and stories.

ACTIVITY

Work with a partner. Write 5 or more names of cartoon movies and the main character in each.

CARTOON MOVIES	CHARACTER
1. *Finding Nemo*	*a fish*
2.	
3.	
4.	
5.	

Share your answers with your classmates. What are the cartoon movies that people know?

WRITING

Write about 3 cartoon (or other) movies. What is the name of each movie? Who is the main character? Did you like it? What other information can you give about each movie?

EXAMPLE:

Finding Nemo is a Walt Disney movie. It is a cartoon movie. The main character is a small fish. I love this movie. The music is great and the characters are funny.

1. _____

_____

2. _____

_____

3. _____

_____

DID YOU KNOW . . . ?
Mickey Mouse's original name was Mortimer. Disney's wife didn't like the name and made her husband change it.

Maya Lin

PREREADING

Answer the questions.

1. How do people remember soldiers who die?
2. What was the Vietnam War?
3. What are some famous war memorials you know about?

Maya Lin

Maya Lin is a famous **architect** today. She is famous for her **design** of the Vietnam Veterans' **Memorial**. This memorial in Washington, D.C., is for **soldiers**. These soldiers died or were missing in the Vietnam War. The Vietnam Veterans' Memorial is the most-visited memorial in the United States.

Maya Lin was an Asian-American student of architecture at Yale University. She took an architecture class with Professor Andrus Burr. At that time, there was a contest for the best design for a memorial for Vietnam veterans. The **contest** was open to all Americans. The prize was $20,000. Professor Burr asked the class to make a design for the Vietnam Veterans' Memorial for homework. Maya got a B for her design. Then Maya, all her classmates, and the professor sent their designs to the contest. One thousand four hundred people sent in their designs.

Some time later, Professor Burr said, " We have the winner for the memorial contest. It is our Maya Lin!" At first, Maya didn't believe the news. It was true! She won, and her professor didn't win! She was only 21 years old. Her design was simple. It was a V-shaped monument. Its walls have the names of 58,175 soldiers.

Lin designed other monuments, too. She continues to design monuments and public **sculptures**.

VOCABULARY

Write the correct word on the line.

~~architect~~	memorial	contest
design	soldiers	sculptures

1. Maya Lin wanted to draw buildings before they were made. She

   wanted to be an ____architect____ .

2. Many _____ went to fight in the war in Vietnam.

3. Maya Lin was the winner of the _____ for the best design.

4. Maya Lin made a drawing, or _____, of the memorial.

5. Maya Lin designs monuments. She also designs figures,

   or _____ .

6. The _____ for the Vietnam Veterans is in Washington, D.C.

COMPREHENSION

⭐ **FOLLOWING THE SEQUENCE**

Number the sentences to show the correct order.

____ Professor Burr asked the class to make a design for the Vietnam
Veterans' Memorial

____ Maya won the contest. She was only 21 years old.

_1_ Maya Lin took an architecture class with Professor Burr.

____ Maya sent her design to the contest.

____ Maya got a B from Professor Burr for her design.

⭐ **LOOKING FOR DETAILS**

Circle *T* if the sentence is true. Circle *F* if the sentence is false.

1. Maya Lin studied architecture at Yale.   (T)   F
2. Twenty thousand people sent their designs for the contest. T   F
3. Professor Burr didn't send his design to the contest.   T   F

4. Maya Lin was 21 years old when she won the contest.　　T　　F
5. Maya's design was a V-shaped monument.　　T　　F

ACTIVITY

Work with a small group. Complete the information on world monuments. Then find 3 more and complete the information.

	CITY/COUNTRY	WHAT IS IT? (tower, wall, bridge, statue, church, tomb, etc.)
Statue of Liberty	New York City, U.S.	statue
Eiffel Tower		
Taj Mahal		
Big Ben		

Share your answers with your classmates. What other world monuments did people find?

WRITING

Write about 2 interesting monuments.

EXAMPLE:

The Pyramid of the Sun is a famous monument in my country, Mexico.

It is in Teotihuacán. This is an ancient Aztec city.

1. _____

_____

2. _____

_____

DID YOU KNOW...?
Maya wanted only the names of the Vietnam Veterans on the wall. Her name is behind the wall where people cannot see it.

Ella Fitzgerald

Answer the questions.

1. Do you like to sing? If so, what kind of music do you sing?
2. Can one day change a person's life? Why?
3. Do you want to change your life? How?

Ella Fitzgerald

Sometimes a person's life changes very quickly. Suddenly, everything is different. Ella Fitzgerald had this kind of life. This is how it began.

Ella lived in an **orphanage** in New York because her parents died. At age 15, she entered a contest in New York. For the contest, she wanted to sing and dance. But Ella was very **nervous** and she could not dance, so she just sang.

Ella did not know the contest was going to change her life. A famous jazz **musician** named Chick Webb was in the **audience**. He was looking for a new singer for his band. When he heard Ella's voice, he gave her the job.

Chick Webb and his wife took care of Ella. They taught her to be a good singer. Ella traveled with his band. In 1938, Ella wrote a song with Chick Webb. This song was a great success. Ella was a **star**.

Chick Webb died, but Ella sang with his band for three more years. Then she sang alone. She traveled all over the world. She had an amazing voice. She could sing any kind of song. People who liked rock music liked her. So did people who liked jazz.

Ella sang for almost 60 years. She sang over 2,000 different songs. She sold over 25 million records and sang with more than 40 **orchestras**. People called her the "First Lady of Song." Ella died in 1996, but people will always remember Ella's voice.

VOCABULARY

Write the correct word on the line.

orphanage	~~musician~~	star
nervous	audience	orchestra

1. Chick Webb was a _____musician_____. He played music and sang songs.

2. Ella was very famous. Everyone knew about her. She was a
   _____.

3. Ella lived with other children who did not have parents. They all lived
   in an _____.

4. Before Ella sang, she was _____. She was scared.

5. A large group of people played music, and Ella sang with them. They
   were the _____.

6. Many people watched Ella sing. They were the _____.

COMPREHENSION

 UNDERSTANDING THE MAIN IDEA

Circle the letter of the best answer.

1. One contest changed Ella's life because ____.
   a. an important person heard her sing
   b. she found a man and woman to take care of her
   c. people saw her dance

2. Ella sang ____.
   a. and danced
   b. only jazz
   c. any kind of song

3. People called Ella the "First Lady of Song" because ____.
   a. she sang with the great musician Chick Webb
   b. she was a famous singer for almost 60 years
   c. she wrote a song and it was a big success

⭐ ## LOOKING FOR DETAILS

Circle *T* if the sentence is true. Circle *F* if the sentence is false.

1. Ella grew up in a famous theater in New York.	T	(F)
2. Ella knew she would be famous after she won a contest.	T	F
3. Chick Webb was famous before Ella was famous.	T	F
4. Webb wanted a new songwriter for his band.	T	F
5. Ella became a star after she wrote a song with Chick Webb.	T	F

ACTIVITY

Talk about the questions with a classmate.

1. What is your favorite kind of music?
2. Who is your favorite male singer?
3. Who is your favorite female singer?
4. Who is your favorite group or band?

Share your answers with your classmates. What kind of music is the most popular? Which performers are most popular?

WRITING

Look at the pictures. Make sentences with the words under the pictures. Write your sentences on the lines.

1. Ella / grew up / orphanage / New York

2. Famous musician Chick Webb / heard / Ella / contest

3. Chick Webb / wanted / Ella / sing / band

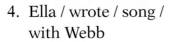

4. Ella / wrote / song /
   with Webb

5. Webb / died / Ella /
   sang / all over world

1. _Ella grew up in an orphanage in New York._

2. _____

3. _____

4. _____

5. _____

DID YOU KNOW . . . ?
Ella Fitzgerald recorded with Louis Armstrong. They both lived in Queens, New York.

PART 7

THE STORY OF YOUNG AMERICA

1492: Christopher Columbus came from Spain. He stopped on an island near America.

In the 1600s: Many British people came and lived in North America. The British king made the laws. The Americans wanted to be free. 1775: The Revolutionary War began.

1783: The British lost the war. The United States was born. George Washington was the first president.

1861: There was a war between the North and the South. It was the Civil War. The war ended in 1865.

1803: President Thomas Jefferson bought land from France.

1869: People built the first railroad across the country.

To quiz yourself about **THE STORY OF YOUNG AMERICA,** *go to page 117.*

Christopher Columbus and the New World

PREREADING

Answer the questions.

1. What nationality was Christopher Columbus?
2. How did people travel in the time of Columbus?
3. What was Christopher Columbus looking for?

Christopher Columbus and the New World

At the time of Columbus, people traveled from Europe to Asia by land. They went to Asia to get silk and **spices**. These things were very **valuable** to Europeans. The trip from Europe to Asia by land was very long and difficult.

Christopher Columbus was born in Genoa, Italy. He loved the sea. He became a **sailor** at age 14. Christopher Columbus had a dream. He wanted to sail to Asia. He thought Asia was across the Atlantic Ocean. He looked for someone to pay for his **trip**.

Many rich people didn't want to help Columbus. They thought Columbus was crazy. Finally, Columbus asked Queen Isabella of Spain to help him. She gave him three ships, sailors, and money for his trip.

Columbus and his sailors were **at sea** for about two months. Finally, they saw land. It was 1492. Columbus thought he was in India. He called the people there "Indians." Later, people understood that Columbus came to a new land and not India. They called this new land the New World. Today, we know that Columbus **landed** on the island which is now the Dominican Republic and Haiti.

VOCABULARY

Write the correct word on the line.

spices	~~sailor~~	at sea
valuable	trip	landed

1. At age 14, Columbus was a _____*sailor*_____ on a ship.

2. Columbus wanted someone to give him money to travel. He wanted someone to pay for his _____.

3. Columbus and his sailors traveled on the ocean. They were _____ for about two months.

4. When the ship came to the island, it _____.

5. People used a lot of _____ like pepper on food to make it tasty.

6. Spices were expensive. They were _____.

COMPREHENSION

⭐ FOLLOWING THE SEQUENCE

Number the sentences to show the correct order.

____ Columbus wanted to sail to Asia.

_1_ Columbus became a sailor at age 14.

____ After two months at sea, Columbus saw land.

____ He thought the land was India. It was 1492.

____ Queen Isabella of Spain gave him 3 ships, sailors, and money.

⭐ LOOKING FOR DETAILS

Circle *T* if the sentence is true. Circle *F* if the sentence is false.

1. Columbus was from Spain.   T   (F)

2. Spices from Asia were expensive.   T   F

3. Queen Isabella gave Columbus only money and sailors for his trip.   T   F

4. Columbus sailed for about two months.   T   F

5. Columbus thought he was in India.   T   F

ACTIVITY

Work in a small group. Complete the chart. What are some things people discovered? What are some things people invented?

DISCOVERIES	INVENTIONS
gold	microwave oven

Share your answers with your classmates. How many different discoveries and inventions did people write in the chart?

WRITING

Think about the story of Christopher Columbus and the New World. Complete the sentences.

1. Europeans traveled to Asia _____ *by land* _____.

2. The trip to Asia _____.

3. Columbus wanted to _____.

4. Columbus thought _____.

5. Queen Isabella _____.

6. In 1492, Columbus _____.

DID YOU KNOW . . . ?

Columbus did not discover America. There were people in what is now America for thousands of years before 1492.

Paul Revere's Ride

PREREADING

Answer the questions.

1. Who is a famous hero in the United States or another country?

2. Why is he or she famous?

3. Do you want to do what this person did? Why?

Paul Revere's Ride

In 1775, people from England lived in **colonies** in America. They were not free. The king in England made the laws. They paid taxes to the king. They did not want to pay money. They wanted to be free. The men got ready to fight the **British**. People called them "Minutemen" because they could be ready to fight in a minute. They **hid** guns in the town of Concord, Massachusetts.

The British soldiers were in Boston. They knew the Americans had guns at Concord. They decided to go to Concord.

Paul Revere was a colonist in Boston. He knew that the British were going to Concord. But Revere did not know how they were going to go. It was important for him to know. He had to tell the Minutemen. Then they could stop the British.

A friend helped Revere. The friend went to the top of a church in Boston. Revere told him to send a **signal**. If the British went on land, show one light. If they went on the Charles River, show two lights. Revere waited. Then he saw two lights. He knew which way the British were going.

Revere crossed the Charles River and **jumped** on a horse. He **rode** very fast. He told the people in the villages that the British soldiers were coming. The Minutemen came to Lexington. They fought the British. The Americans won. This was the first fight of the American Revolution.

VOCABULARY

Write the correct word on the line.

colonies	hid	jumped
British	~~signal~~	rode

1. Revere's friend showed two lights. This _____*signal*_____ told Revere something.

2. Paul Revere _____ a horse to Lexington.

3. The people in America were not free. They lived in _____.

4. Paul Revere was watching for the signal. He saw the two lights. He crossed the river and _____ up on a horse.

5. The Minutemen _____ their guns. They did not want the British to find the guns.

6. The people from England are the _____.

COMPREHENSION

⭐ FOLLOWING THE SEQUENCE

Number the sentences to show the correct order.

____ Paul Revere's friend helped him and sent him a signal.

____ The Americans won.

_1_ Paul Revere wanted to tell the Minutemen the British were coming.

____ The Minutemen came and fought the British.

____ When he got the signal, he crossed the river, jumped on a horse, and rode fast.

⭐ LOOKING FOR DETAILS

Complete each sentence with the correct word or words. Write the letter of your answer on the line.

1. The Minutemen hid guns in __c__.
2. Paul Revere was an American ____.
3. Revere's friend sent a signal from ____.
4. Revere told the colonists, ____.
5. The first fight of the American Revolution was in ____.

a. the top of a church
b. the British soldiers were coming
c̶. Concord
d. Lexington
e. colonist

ACTIVITY

Talk with a partner. Why do people today pay taxes? Which taxes are good? Which are bad? Share your answers with your classmates. Which taxes are good? Which taxes are bad? Why?

WRITING

Write about 4 important events in your life. Why were they important?

> **EXAMPLE:**
> _My first day in school was important because my family was new in town and I didn't know anyone._

1. _____
2. _____
3. _____
4. _____

DID YOU KNOW . . . ?
Paul Revere was a silversmith. He had 16 children.

The Railroad Connects East and West

PREREADING

Answer the questions.

1. How did people travel in the United States before cars and trains?

2. How long do you think it took to build a railroad from coast to coast?

3. How many people do you think worked to build the railroad?

The Railroad Connects East and West

The first settlers in the United States lived mainly on the East **coast**. By 1860, there were many more people on the West coast of the United States, too. At that time, people usually used horses to travel. It is 3,000 miles from the East to the West. This was a long way on horses. The people in the West were **cut off** from people in the East. Letters took about two months. Sometimes they never arrived.

The government decided to build a railroad to connect the East and the West. There were two companies to build the railroad: the Union Pacific Company and the Central Pacific Company. One company started to build in the East. The other started in the West. The two companies met in the middle to make one railroad.

The government gave **prizes**. For every mile of railroad, the company received 12,800 acres of free land on both sides of the railway. Both companies worked hard. Each company used over 10,000 workers. The Central Pacific railroad had a more difficult job. The builders worked on high mountains and made **tunnels** through them. The work was hard and very dangerous. They **hired** Chinese workers. The Chinese worked harder than the other workers.

In 1869, after 7 years, the two railroads met in the state of Utah. It was a very important moment. There were celebrations. The railroad connected East and West **at last**.

VOCABULARY

Write the correct word on the line.

coast	prizes	hired
cut off	~~tunnels~~	at last

1. The builders made _____*tunnels*_____ to go through the mountains.

2. Finally the two railroads joined the East and the West. They were joined _____.

3. The people in the East were _____ from the people in the West. It was difficult for them to communicate with each other.

4. The Central Pacific Company paid many Chinese workers for work. The company _____ Chinese workers.

5. The government gave gifts or _____ to the railroad company.

6. The East of the United States by the ocean is the East _____.

COMPREHENSION

 UNDERSTANDING THE MAIN IDEA

Circle the letter of the best answer.

1. The East and the West of the United States were ____.

   a. dangerous places

   b. cut off from each other

   c. the only places with horses

2. The government ____ to build a railroad to connect East and West.

   a. did not want

   b. had one company

   c. wanted

3. The two railroads ____.

   a. liked each other

   b. connected in Utah

   c. hired Chinese workers

LOOKING FOR DETAILS

Circle *T* if the sentence is true. Circle *F* if the sentence is false.

1. It took 2 months for a letter to get from the
   East to the West coast.   Ⓣ   F
2. The total number of workers on the railroads
   was 10,000.   T   F
3. The Central Pacific hired Chinese workers.   T   F
4. The railroad took 7 years to build.   T   F
5. The Union Pacific had a longer and more difficult job.   T   F

ACTIVITY

Work with a partner. Complete the chart. Write 5 forms of transportation under *Transportation*. Choose 1 or more adjectives from the box to describe each form of transportation.

cheap	convenient	expensive	not comfortable	safe
comfortable	dangerous	fast	private	slow

TRANSPORTATION	ADJECTIVE
1. *buses*	*cheap, convenient, slow*
2.	
3.	
4.	
5.	

Share your answers with your classmates. What kinds of transportation do people like the most? The least?

WRITING

Write about 1 form of transportation you like and 1 form of
transportation you don't like. Give 3 reasons for each one.

EXAMPLE:

I like cars. They are expensive, but cars are convenient, private, and

comfortable.

I don't like bicycles. They are cheap, but they are not comfortable. You

get wet in the rain. You cannot take big bags with you.

_____

_____

_____

_____

_____

DID YOU KNOW . . . ?

The Native Americans didn't like the railroad on their land. They called it
"The Iron Horse." They often attacked the trains.

Fill in the blanks with the information from the map and *U.S. Facts* on pages 2–3.

1. There are _____ states in the United States.

2. About _____ million people live in the United States.

3. _____ is the capital city of the United States.

4. _____ is the largest state.

5. The longest river is the _____.

6. Olympia is the state capital of _____.

7. The Mississippi River starts in _____.

8. The Grand Canyon is in _____.

9. The highest mountain is in _____.

10. Hawaii is in the _____ Ocean.

11. _____ was the first state.

12. The Golden Gate Bridge is in the state of _____.

13. Mount Rushmore is in _____.

14. There are 10,000 lakes in _____.

15. The Kennedy Space Center is in _____.

16. _____ was the 50th state.

17. Oranges grow in _____.

18. Corn grows in _____.

19. The United States has more _____, _____, and
    _____ than any other country.

20. Austin is in _____.

21. Potatoes grow in _____.

22. Texas has cattle and _____.

23. Cheese comes from _____.

24. Pineapples grow in _____.

Check your answers in the Answer Key on page 122.

QUIZ 2

....

Fill in the blanks with the information from *U.S. Inventions and Inventors* on pages 18–19.

1. Samuel Morse invented the _____.

2. _____ developed the polio vaccine.

3. Orville and Wilbur Wright flew the first _____.

4. Vladimir Zworykin invented the _____.

5. _____ invented the phonograph.

6. Josephine Cochrane invented the _____.

7. Igor Sikorsky built the _____.

8. Alexander Graham Bell invented the _____.

9. _____ invented bifocal lenses for eyeglasses.

10. Charles Duryea and J. Frank Duryea invented the first

     _____.

11. Percy Spencer invented the _____.

12. Chester Carlson invented _____.

13. George Eastman produced the _____ camera.

14. _____ invented the laser for cataracts.

15. Isaac Singer invented the _____.

Check your answers in the Answer Key on page 122.

QUIZ 3

. . . .

Fill in the blanks with the information from *U.S. Originals* on pages 34–35.

1. Levi _____ made the first jeans.

2. Three friends opened a coffee shop and started _____.

3. Mr. and Mrs. Wallace started the magazine _____.

4. A druggist invented _____ in Atlanta, Georgia.

5. William _____ made flavored chewing gum.

6. W.W. Kellogg made _____.

7. Dr. John Harvey Kellogg in St.Louis invented a machine to make

   _____.

8. The tuxedo got its name from _____, New York.

9. King _____ made razors safe.

10. Jerry Siegel and Joe Shuster wrote the story of _____.

11. Arthur Wayne published the first _____ in a newspaper.

12. Two brothers sold the restaurant _____.

Check your answers in the Answer Key on page 122.

Fill in the blanks with information from *Holidays and Special Days* on pages 50–51.

1. New Year's Day is on _____.

2. Mexicans celebrate _____ on May 5.

3. Families get together and have a big dinner on _____.

4. The birthday of the United States is on _____. It is _____ Day.

5. The _____ is in January or February.

6. _____ is Valentine's Day.

7. Children wear costumes on _____.

8. Veterans Day is on _____.

9. Irish Americans celebrate _____ on March 17.

10. People remember the African-American leader _____ in January.

11. Jewish people celebrate _____ in December.

12. People give gifts on _____.

13. People remember George Washington and Abraham Lincoln on _____.

14. People celebrate the old and the new on _____.

15. Americans remember people who died in U.S. wars on _____.

16. People remember American workers on _____.

Check your answers in the Answer Key on page 122.

QUIZ 5

Fill in the blanks with the information from *Washington, D.C.* on pages 64–65.

1. Washington, D.C., is the _____ of the United States.

2. The president lives in the _____.

3. Almost 200,000 U.S. soldiers have graves in _____.

4. The offices of the U.S. Army, Navy, Air Force, Marines, and Coast Guard are in the _____.

5. The _____ is the largest museum in the world.

6. Congress meets in the _____ building.

7. Members of Congress make _____ for the country.

8. The _____ is the world's largest library.

9. 1791: _____ chose the place for the capital city.

10. 1814: The _____ burned the White House, the Capitol, and other buildings.

11. 1963: _____ gave a famous speech at the Lincoln Memorial.

12. 1912: _____ gave the United States 3,000 cherry trees.

13. The American flag is sometimes called _____.

Check your answers in the Answer Key on page 122.

QUIZ 6

Fill in the blanks with the information from *U.S. Arts and Entertainment* on pages 80–81.

1. Frank Lloyd Wright was an _____.

2. Emily Dickinson was a _____.

3. Maya _____ writes about her childhood.

4. Isamu Noguchi's _____ are very modern.

5. Steven Spielberg is a _____.

6. _____ books are about life on the river.

7. Georgia O'Keeffe's paintings are of _____ and landscapes.

8. Maya Lin is famous for the _____.

9. _____ was a jazz trumpet player.

10. People called _____ the "First Lady of Song."

11. Disneyland gets its name from _____.

12. Langston Hughes is famous for his _____.

Check your answers in the Answer Key on page 122.

QUIZ 7

Fill in the blanks with information from *The Story of Young America* on pages 96–97.

1. 1492: _____ landed on an island near America.

2. The people in America wanted to be free from _____.

3. _____: The Revolutionary War began.

4. 1783: The United States was _____.

5. _____ was the first president.

6. 1803: _____ bought land from France.

7. 1869: People built a railroad _____ the country.

8. _____: The Civil War between the North and the South began.

Check your answers in the Answer Key on page 122.

ANSWER KEY

UNIT 1

VOCABULARY

2. alligator   3. sandy beaches
4. theme park   5. astronauts
6. palm trees

UNDERSTANDING THE MAIN IDEA

1. a   2. b

LOOKING FOR DETAILS

2. c   3. b   4. a   5. e

ACTIVITY

Answers will vary.

WRITING

Answers will vary.

UNIT 2

VOCABULARY

2. salmon   3. cutdown   4. smoke
5. forest   6. volcanoes

UNDERSTANDING THE MAIN IDEA

1. b   1. a

LOOKING FOR DETAILS

2. F   3. F   4. F   5. T

ACTIVITY

Answers will vary.

WRITING

Answers will vary.

UNIT 3

VOCABULARY

2. lakes   3. pancakes   4. syrup
5. buckets   6. A gallon

UNDERSTANDING THE MAIN IDEA

1. b   2. c

LOOKING FOR DETAILS

2. F   3. T   4. T   5. T

ACTIVITY

Answers will vary.

WRITING

Answers will vary.

UNIT 4

VOCABULARY

2. became   3. melted   4. noticed
5. exploded   6. weighed

UNDERSTANDING THE MAIN IDEA

1. b   2. a

LOOKING FOR DETAILS

2. popped → melted
3. tons → pounds
4. brown → white
5. four → three

ACTIVITY

Answers will vary.

WRITING

2. One day, Spencer stopped in front of a magnetron.
3. The chocolate bar in his pocket melted.
4. He put popcorn next to the magnetron.
5. Popcorn popped everywhere in the laboratory.
6. Spencer had an idea.

UNIT 5

VOCABULARY

2. saucers   3. company   4. servants
5. lovely   6. broke

FOLLOWING THE SEQUENCE

2. 1, 2   3. 2, 1   4. 2, 1   5. 1, 2

LOOKING FOR DETAILS

2. b   3. a   4. a   5. b

ACTIVITY

Answers will vary.

WRITING

Answers will vary.

UNIT 6

VOCABULARY

2. cataract   3. remove   4. painful
5. accurate   6. equipment

UNDERSTANDING THE MAIN IDEA

1. b   2. c

LOOKING FOR DETAILS

2. free → easy
3. students → free
4. surgery → care
5. cataracts → blindness

ACTIVITY

Answers will vary.

WRITING

Answers will vary.

UNIT 7

VOCABULARY

2. borrowed   3. disappointed
4. milk shakes   5. enough   6. waited in line

FOLLOWING THE SEQUENCE

2. 2, 1   3. 2, 1   4. 2, 1   5. 1, 2

LOOKING FOR DETAILS

2. salads → French fries
3. Boston → Chicago
4. 3.5 → 2.5
5. unhappy → happy

ACTIVITY

Answers will vary.

WRITING

2. They called the restaurant McDonald's.

3. They had three things on the menu.
4. People waited in line outside the restaurant.
5. Ray Kroc went to California to see Mc Donald's.
6. The brothers sold McDonald's to Ray Kroc.

UNIT 8

VOCABULARY

2. lucky   3. situation   4. hero
5. ordinary   6. comic books

COMPREHENSION

2. a   3. b   4. e

LOOKING FOR DETAILS

2. F   3. F   4. F   5. T

ACTIVITY

Answers will vary.

WRITING

Answers will vary.

UNIT 9

VOCABULARY

2. a trip   3. kept the name   4. flavors
5. Italian-style   6. coffee beans

FOLLOWING THE SEQUENCE

2. 1, 2   3. 2, 1   4. 2, 1   5. 2, 1

LOOKING FOR DETAILS

2. 1981 → 1971
3. made → sold
4. cups → beans
5. country → world

ACTIVITY

Answers will vary.

WRITING

Answers will vary.

UNIT 10

VOCABULARY

2. celebration   3. blow horns   4. crowd
5. ring bells   6. parade

UNDERSTANDING THE MAIN IDEA

1. c   2. a

LOOKING FOR DETAILS

2. F   3. F   4. F   5. T

ACTIVITY

Answers will vary.

WRITING

Answers will vary.

UNIT 11

VOCABULARY

2. Ireland → country
3. green → color
4. shamrock → plant
5. priest → religious person; works in a church
6. Chicago → city

UNDERSTANDING THE MAIN IDEA

1. b   2. a   3. b

LOOKING FOR DETAILS

2. e   3. b   4. c   5. a

ACTIVITY

Answers will vary.

WRITING

Answers will vary.

UNIT 12

VOCABULARY

2. lose   3. benefits   4. factories
5. picnic   6. labor unions

FOLLOWING THE SEQUENCE

2. 2, 1   3. 1, 2   4. 2, 1

LOOKING FOR DETAILS

2. F   3. F   4. T   5. T

ACTIVITY

Answers will vary.

WRITING

Answers will vary.

UNIT 13

VOCABULARY

2. staff   3. barbershop   4. elect
5. statue   6. pass laws

COMPREHENSION

2. d   3. a   4. b

LOOKING FOR DETAILS

2. F   3. T   4. T   5. F

ACTIVITY

Answers will vary.

WRITING

Answers will vary.

UNIT 14

VOCABULARY

2. objects   3. flag   4. selected
5. galleries   6. popular

FOLLOWING THE SEQUENCE

2. 2, 1   3. 1, 2   4. 2, 1   5. 1, 2

LOOKING FOR DETAILS

2. a   3. d   4. e   5. b

ACTIVITY

Answers will vary.

WRITING

Answers will vary.

UNIT 15

VOCABULARY

2. astronaut   3. guard   4. tomb
5. flame   6. monument

UNDERSTANDING THE MAIN IDEA

1. c   2. c   3. b

LOOKING FOR DETAILS

2. 5,000 → 2,000
3. statue → flame
4. soldiers → astronauts
5. president → guard

ACTIVITY

Answers will vary.

WRITING

Answers will vary.

UNIT 16

VOCABULARY

2. characters   3. draw   4. cartoonist
5. actors   6. huge

FOLLOWING THE SEQUENCE

2. 2, 1   3. 2, 1   4. 1, 2   5. 2, 1

LOOKING FOR DETAILS

2. newspaper → movie
3. cartoons → actors
4. movie → success
5. actors → characters

ACTIVITY

Answers will vary.

WRITING

Answers will vary.

UNIT 17

VOCABULARY

2. soldiers   3. contest   4. design
5. sculptures   6. memorial

FOLLOWING THE SEQUENCE

2, 5, 1, 4, 3

LOOKING FOR DETAILS

2. F   3. F   4. T   5. T

ACTIVITY

Answers will vary.

WRITING

Answers will vary.

UNIT 18

VOCABULARY

2. star   3. orphanage   4. nervous
5. orchestra   6. audience

UNDERSTANDING THE MAIN IDEA

1. a   2. c   3. b

LOOKING FOR DETAILS

2. F   3. T   4. F   5. T

ACTIVITY

Answers will vary.

WRITING

2. Famous musician Chick Webb heard Ella sing in a contest.
3. Chick Webb wanted Ella to sing with his band.
4. Ella wrote a song with Webb.
5. After Chick Webb died, Ella sang all over the world.

UNIT 19

VOCABULARY

2. trip   3. at sea   4. landed   5. spices
6. valuable

FOLLOWING THE SEQUENCE

2, 1, 4, 5, 3

LOOKING FOR DETAILS

2. T   3. F   4. T   5. T

ACTIVITY

Answers will vary.

WRITING

2. was very long and difficult.
3. sail to Asia.
4. he was in India.
5. gave Columbus (him) three ships, sailors, and money for his trip.
6. Answers will vary, but some possible answers are: sailed across the Atlantic Ocean; landed in a new land; left Spain for India.

UNIT 20

VOCABULARY

2. rode   3. colonies   4. jumped
5. hid   6. British

FOLLOWING THE SEQUENCE

2, 5, 1, 4, 3

LOOKING FOR DETAILS

2. e   3. a   4. b   5. d

ACTIVITY

Answers will vary.

WRITING

Answers will vary.

UNIT 21

VOCABULARY

2. at last   3. cut off   4. hired
5. prizes   6. coast

UNDERSTANDING THE MAIN IDEA

1. b   2. c   3. b

LOOKING FOR DETAILS

2. F   3. T   4. T   5. F

ACTIVITY

Answers will vary.

WRITING

Answers will vary.

QUIZ 1

1. fifty   2. 300 million   3. Washington, D. C.
4. Alaska   5. Mississippi   6. Washington
7. Minnesota   8. Arizona   9. Alaska
10. Pacific   11. Delaware   12. California
13. South Dakota   14. Minnesota
15. Florida   16. Hawaii   17. Florida
18. Iowa   19. corn, beef, and milk
20. Texas   21. Idaho   22. oil
23. Wisconsin   24. Hawaii

QUIZ 2

1. telegraph   2. Jonas Salk
3. motor airplane   4. TV   5. Thomas Edison
6. dishwasher   7. helicopter   8. telephone
9. Benjamin Franklin
10. gasoline automobile
11. the microwave oven
12. Xerox machine   13. Kodak
14. Patricia Bath   15. sewing machine

QUIZ 3

1. Strauss   2. Starbucks   3. Reader's Digest
4. Coca Cola   5. Wrigley   6. corn flakes
7. peanut butter   8. Tuxedo Park   9. Gillette
10. Superman   11. crossword puzzle
12. McDonald's

QUIZ 4

1. January 1   2. Cinco de Mayo
3. Thanksgiving   4. July 4th, Independence
5. Chinese New Year   6. February 14th
7. Halloween   8. November 11th
9. St. Patrick's Day   10. Martin Luther King
11. Hanukkah   12. Christmas
13. President's Day   14. New Year's Eve
15. Memorial Day   16. Labor Day

QUIZ 5

1. capital city   2. White House
3. Arlington National Cemetery   4. Pentagon
5. Smithsonian Institution   6. Capitol
7. laws   8. Library of Congress
9. George Washington   10. British
11. Martin Luther King   12. Japan
13. The Stars and Stripes

QUIZ 6

1. architect   2. poet   3. Angelou
4. sculptures   5. movie director
6. Mark Twain's   7. flowers
8. Vietnam Veterans' Memorial
9. Louis Armstrong   10. Ella Fitzgerald
11. Walt Disney   12. poetry

QUIZ 7

1. Christopher Columbus
2. England or Britain   3. 1775   4. born
5. George Washington   6. Thomas Jefferson
7. across   8. 1861

AUDIO CD TRACKING LIST

Track	Activity	Page
1	Audio Program Introduction	
2	**UNIT 1:** Florida	5
3	**UNIT 2:** Washington	10
4	**UNIT 3:** Vermont	15
5	**UNIT 4:** Spencer's Microwave Oven	21
6	**UNIT 5:** Josephine Cochrane's Dishwasher	26
7	**UNIT 6:** Patricia Bath's Laser	31
8	**UNIT 7:** McDonald's	37
9	**UNIT 8:** Superman	42
10	**UNIT 9:** Starbucks	46
11	**UNIT 10:** New Year's Celebrations	53
12	**UNIT 11:** St. Patrick's Day	57
13	**UNIT 12:** Labor Day	61
14	**UNIT 13:** The Capitol	67
15	**UNIT 14:** The Smithsonian Institution	71
16	**UNIT 15:** Arlington National Cemetery	76
17	**UNIT 16:** Walt Disney	83
18	**UNIT 17:** Maya Lin	88
19	**UNIT 18:** Ella Fitzgerald	92
20	**UNIT 19:** Christopher Columbus and the New World	99
21	**UNIT 20:** Paul Revere's Ride	103
22	**UNIT 21:** The Railroad Connects East and West	107